THE SCHOOL OF INTENTIONAL LIVING

A REAL-WORLD APPROACH TO LIVING LIFE ON YOUR TERMS

SEAN ROSENSTEEL

THE SCHOOL OF INTENTIONAL LIVING

A Real-World Approach to Living Life on Your Terms

ISBNs:

978-1-7351789-0-5 *Hardcover*

978-1-7351789-4-3 *Paperback*

978-1-7351789-2-9 *Ebook*

978-1-7351789-3-6 *Audiobook*

Cover design by Jelena Mirkovic Jankovic

DOWNLOAD THE AUDIOBOOK FREE!

To express my sincere appreciation for buying my book, I would like to give you the Audiobook version 100% FREE!

TO DOWNLOAD GO TO:

SeanRosensteel.com/intentional-audiobook

For my parents, who never gave up on me.

TABLE OF CONTENTS

INTRODUCTION: WHY CONVENTIONAL WISDOM IS A TRAP

"What if my whole life has been wrong?"

— IVAN ILYCH

These words, spoken in the final moments by Ivan himself in Leo Tolstoy's famous novel *The Death of Ivan Ilych*, have haunted me for many years.

I'll bet these words haunt you a little, too.

If so, I'm going to make a bold assumption: you've trusted *conventional wisdom* to guide certain aspects of your life.

I'll bet you went to school in the hope it would provide you with everything you needed to be "successful" in the *real world*. You earned a high school or college degree so you could land a decent job or start a business. With some steady income, you bought a home. Maybe you settled down and started a family of your own. For as long as you can remember, you've always believed that working hard for several decades would earn you the right to one day enjoy a comfortable retirement.

The problem with blindly following conventional wisdom is *one day* may never come.

After some time, many of us wake up and take a hard look in the mirror. We begin to realize we're not where we want to be. We wish we were further along. We thought we'd have better health, more wealth and deeper relationships at this stage in our lives. There's this nagging feeling that *something is missing*.

We've been drifting for so many years, we're now feeling a bit lost. Going through the motions no longer satisfies us. With a subtle sense of uncertainty, we come to the realization that there's more to life than we've previously noted.

We have this longing to live more *intentionally*. We have this desire to make more of a difference in the lives of those we lead, love and serve. The problem, of course, is that the hourglass of life is now working against us. We're afraid that if we don't make a change soon, we may never reach our true potential as human and spiritual beings.

Some people call this a "quarter" or "mid-life" crisis. Carl Jung, the great Swiss psychiatrist who founded analytical psychology, referred to this as the "afternoon" of our lives.[1] In his book *The Shift*, Wayne Dyer describes this as a time in our lives when we move from a place of ambition to a place of meaning.[2]

In the meantime, we've picked up an enormous amount of responsibility along the way. Some of us have soul-crushing jobs or businesses that demand our around-the-clock attention. Expenses are steadily increasing, the mortgage is due and there are numerous mouths to feed. Our loved ones aren't getting any younger, and they will soon, if not already, require extra care.

Every day we're being pulled in all sorts of directions. It feels like everything and everyone demands our attention. We're spread thin and stress levels are shooting through the roof. Our lives become a never-ending state of imbalance, spiraling out of control. Despite our good intentions to live more *intentionally*, we're not sure where we'll find the time in our busy schedules to make that happen.

So how, then, do we approach this subject of intentional living?

No one ever taught us this. No one ever taught us how to live our lives based on our own unique definitions of success. We didn't learn it from our parents, our society or our culture. Religious institutions don't teach this, and the formal education system doesn't either.

While all of these influential sources have certainly contributed in meaningful ways, we're still left wondering how to start living intentionally based on all the unique circumstances with which we now find ourselves surrounded.

A Real-World Approach

In the following pages, you'll find a real-world approach that helps you break free from conventional wisdom and pursue your own definition of success. It's a practical approach that will meet you where you are and support you based on your unique circumstances. It will help you navigate this incredibly fun and rewarding journey into intentional living. No matter where you're looking to go, this book will help you get there, even if you don't know where *there* is just yet.

Best of all, this isn't proprietary. In fact, I'll bet you're already familiar with every single element within this simple approach.

Before going into further detail, I'm going to ask you to use your imagination for a moment.

Imagine waking up one day in the not-so-distant future. You look in the mirror, and you have this *internal knowing* that you're on the right path.

This new version of you has discovered what truly matters most. You've objectively assessed your entire life, and for once, you're finally organized around your highest priorities.

You've made the shift from living reactively to living proactively. You're more effective than ever before with your time, and you're making the most of each day.

The people you love, lead and serve begin to notice your transformation.

You're no longer distracted with the things that used to steal your attention away from the present. Instead, you're laser-focused.

You've envisioned a compelling future for your life by defining clear and meaningful goals. With this new sense of clarity, procrastination is a thing of the past. You're experiencing significant progress in every area of your life, and you're finally advancing in the direction of your dreams.

You're taking time out of your busy schedule to course-correct along the way. You're succeeding faster than ever before, and you've taken your learning and growth to an entirely new level.

This might seem like a far-fetched fantasy, but I'm here to tell you it's not.

Who Am I to Teach this Subject?

I'm *obsessed* with living intentionally, but I wasn't always this way.

To say I was living *unintentionally* for the first three decades of my life would be quite the understatement.

My wife often jokes that I was born with nine lives. For starters, as an infant I almost suffocated to death due to an allergic reaction. When I was no longer breathing and my skin had turned blue, my mother decided it was time to rush me to the emergency room (yet another one I owe you for, Mom).

As a teenager, I often carried around an immortal attitude. I frequently participated in what became known as the "pass out" game. The winners of this careless competition experience what it's like to pass out from a lack of oxygen to the brain. When you win, your friends observe, laugh for a few seconds, and then desperately hope you'll wake up from your temporary slumber.

I was fortunate enough to walk away from a high-speed car crash during my senior year in high school. My friend and I slid in a convertible at a speed of over 100MPH straight into a telephone pole. Luckily for me, my friend became my guardian angel that night. He told me to put my seatbelt on when the car surpassed the 85MPH threshold, just moments before impact.

Growing up, I admired a role model who used tobacco. Doing everything in my power to follow his lead, I decided it would be cool if I tried it, too. Despite incessantly using tobacco for fifteen years straight, I consider myself incredibly lucky to have a clean bill of health.

I've blacked out on hundreds of occasions after consuming excessive amounts of alcohol. Even though I was arrested numerous times due to my intoxicated behavior, I never had the desire to quit. Not even an intervention held by my roommates during my senior year in college could stop me from abusing the substance. You know you've hit a low when the leader of the intervention, known around campus as the "naked cowboy," tells you *you* have the problem.

In one of the most drunken and selfish moments of my life, I swallowed a lethal dose of sleeping pills before passing out one night. I wish I could tell you what I was thinking, but I can't. I suppose I was in so much pain, and so confused while in this inebriated state, I figured it was best to never wake up to see the light of the next day.

Some might say I'm a slow learner, and they'd probably be right, but eventually I did wake up, both literally and figuratively.

My (Literally) Bankrupt Marriage

The wake-up call that finally got my attention occurred just thirty days before my wedding.

I went bankrupt.

This was a truly transformational event, as it caused me to examine my life for the very first time.

I bet you've experienced one of these transformational moments in your life, too. Sometimes these moments have a tendency to shift our personal values and beliefs in an extraordinary way. They can completely alter the trajectory of our future, making the previous "template" from which we were living our lives obsolete.

The blessing of bankruptcy had this effect on me. It helped me realize that finances were the least of my concerns: I was physically, emotionally and spiritually bankrupt as well. Hell, even my relationships were bankrupt.

At a very young age, I adopted what you might call a "conventional" definition of success. In my early twenties, I was buying things I couldn't afford in the hope of impressing others and keeping up with the Joneses: a big home, fast cars, fancy toys. Some people own these things for the right reasons, but not me. I was searching for a false sense of identity and fulfillment from these material possessions.

My emotional state was in ruins. I frequently abused alcohol to escape the mental prison I had created for myself. I was also using tobacco as a means of overcoming my boredom and numbing my nerves.

After many years of this selfish and careless behavior, I grew more and more distant from the people in my life who mattered the most: my parents, my siblings and my closest friends. Furthermore, I had abandoned all communication with my higher power.

Yet there I stood, on the verge of walking down the aisle and committing the rest of my life to the woman I loved.

My fiancé often shared her life-long dream with me throughout our engagement. Ever since she was a little girl, she always knew she wanted to become a loving mother and raise a family of her own.

I began questioning whether I was the right person for her. Was I capable of supporting her in making this dream a reality? Why did she think I was "the one?" How could someone like me become a responsible husband and father figure when I hadn't yet learned how to take responsibility for my own life?

What I didn't realize back then was this:

She believed in me during a time when I didn't believe in myself.

I'll be forever grateful to her for giving me the gift of confidence, a gift that I was incapable of giving myself at that time.

My Parents Are Going to Kill Me

One train of thought led to the next as I continued my self-examination. I suddenly realized how disappointed my parents would be when they found out I went bankrupt.

Not only had they blessed me with their unconditional love, but they had always supported me financially as well. They had invested their hard-earned money in my education; sixteen years' worth of private education to be exact. They even lent me some money shortly after I graduated college to help me get settled into the "real world."

When my attorney asked me if I wanted to include the money I had borrowed from my parents in the bankruptcy, I negligently said yes. There was nothing I could do to change that now.

I pictured my mother walking across the street to grab the day's mail. As she flipped through all the junk, a letter from the government would catch her eye. She would anxiously open it, not sure whether it was real or a scam. Shock and disbelief would sink in as she realized her son had discharged the money he owed to her in a federal court of law.

I paused just long enough to let the feeling sink in. I had *failed* at this thing called life.

I figured the least I could do was warn her. What I didn't realize was that this phone call would forever change my life.

Shortly after she answered my call, my dad hopped on the line, too. There was a long pause after I nervously delivered the news. Eagerly awaiting their response, I translated their silence as utter disappointment.

What they said next wasn't profound. In fact, if they said these words to me once, they said them a hundred times, but this time, I heard their words for the *first* time.

My dad, in his low and direct tone, said, "Sean, no one is responsible for you but you."

My mom, in her loving, nurturing tone, said, "It's time to find a quiet place and figure things out for yourself."

So that's exactly what I did.

Learning to Live Intentionally

Thanks to this guidance from my folks, at twenty-eight years old I finally took charge of my life and began to "figure things out" for myself.

Looking back, my transformation was quite simple. First, I developed a greater awareness of the areas of my life requiring drastic improvement (this wasn't difficult as I needed a total life makeover). Then, when the timing made sense, I went in search of the right solutions. Shortly after applying what I had learned, I began to see positive results.

I was doing something I had come to despise during my formal education years: *learning.* Unlike my experiences in school, what I was learning was actually *relevant.* Some people might call this personal development; I call it self-education. I read books, enrolled in online courses and attended as many live events as I could afford.

Eventually, I became *obsessed* with this idea of intentional living.

Over time, what I found wasn't a miracle drug, religion or a guru. Instead, I simply discovered a practical approach that helps me live more intentionally. An approach that guides me in living my life based on *my own* definition of success.

Getting Lucky

I've had a lot of good fortune since then, leading me to finally answer that wake-up call nearly ten years ago.

I've reconnected to my higher power in a deep, profound way. I've become mentally stronger, replacing limiting thought patterns with more empowering ones. Alcohol and tobacco no longer rule my choices. I'm healthier now and in the best shape of my life. My wife and I are looking forward to celebrating ten years of marriage this year, and we've been blessed with three beautiful children along the way. More open, honest and authentic relationships have been reignited with family and friends. My wife and I have started a few businesses together, one of which was recently acquired. My financial affairs are finally in order. I volunteer often with my children, and I'm blessed to serve on the board of a charity I care deeply about.

I share this with you in the hope it will convey the effectiveness of the approach I've been using. This is the approach I wish someone would have taught me ten years ago, and it's the same approach that continues to guide my life today.

Still "Playing Small"

Meanwhile, I still feel like I'm holding back and "playing small" in certain areas of my life.

I still don't connect with my higher power as often as I'd like. I still get stressed, frustrated and say things I'm not proud of when I'm angry. I still scour the pantry and grab that bag of chips after 8:00 p.m. Certain problems still keep me awake, staring at the ceiling at 2:00 a.m. I've already skipped a few exercise routines this month. I still forget that sometimes my wife simply needs an ear to listen instead of a brain to problem solve. I'm still guilty of losing my patience with my children when I return home from work during what we call the "witching hour" in our home. I still go for long stretches at a time without checking in with my loved ones as often as I'd like. I thought I'd be much further along in my career by now. My financial picture is okay, but I wish it were better.

I'm still dealing with the same "real world" pressures everyone else deals with. I still feel the dense weight of all the responsibility I've accumulated on my shoulders. Sometimes it feels like it's impossible to balance it all.

But there's a big difference: despite the fact that life isn't "perfect," I feel wildly *fulfilled*.

I'm sincerely grateful for each and every day that's gifted to me. I have this peace of mind, this *internal knowing*, that I'm on the right path. I'm so appreciative of all the efforts, all the struggles and all the progress I've experienced thus far in my life.

For nearly ten years now, I've been living intentionally based on *my* definition of success.

Teaching Others

Soon after discovering this approach and experiencing such positive results, family members, close friends and even clients began to take notice. To my surprise, some of them asked me if I was willing to teach them this approach.

This was humbling, and at first, I wasn't sure. What do I know? Who am I to teach the subject of intentional living? How would

I ever put this into a teachable format? What if it doesn't work for them as well as it works for me?

Every time I thought about teaching this to others, my brain would come up with more and more reasons as to why it wouldn't work.

Thankfully, the requests kept coming. Rather than looking at these requests from a selfish perspective, I began looking at them as opportunities to contribute to others in my own unique way. I eventually organized this approach into what is now a series of practical, actionable steps.

Over the past five years, I've had the good fortune of teaching this approach to multitudes of individuals and groups from all over the country. The youngest person I taught was a sixteen-year-old female in high school. The oldest? A seventy-two-year-old male. Both shared a common desire to live a more intentional life, and both experienced a significant transformation as a result of adopting this approach.

I also received many suggestions to write a book. As an avid reader, I've always had such great respect for the many authors I've learned from. Isn't their ability to organize and clarify their thoughts around a specific subject incredible? I didn't think I could ever do this. The project itself seemed too daunting. I also found it hard to grasp the subject matter itself. How could someone write a book on a topic like intentional living in a way that would be relatable to the reader?

Thanks to the many suggestions I received over the years, the seed to write a book was planted. Sure enough, like most seeds you nurture over time, this one eventually blossomed.

An Idea Whose Time Has Come

Viktor Hugo, one of the great poets and novelists of the 19th century, once said, "All the forces in the world are not so powerful as an idea whose time has come."

Months ago, an idea struck me like a bolt of lightning during a deep meditation. This single idea was so powerful that it compelled me to alter the direction of my career and set out to write the very book you are reading today.

Here's the idea:

Every single element within this approach to intentional living was directly influenced by the formal education system.

This certainly isn't a profound idea. In fact, it angered me the moment it reached my awareness.

For as long as I can remember, I always believed my formal education was a complete waste of time. I never took what I learned in school very seriously because I didn't see how it applied in the "real world." This idea challenged the very beliefs I had acquired through my own personal experience.

Furthermore, it threatened the approach I thought *I* had developed. It suggested that *my* brainchild had been directly influenced by my experiences in school. I needed to give credit where credit was due, and my ego didn't appreciate that very much.

After doing everything in my power to discredit this idea, I eventually gave in. It was simply too powerful to ignore. As I began opening up to it and thinking about the possibilities, the entire subject matter unfolded beautifully.

This was exactly what I had been searching for all along:

An entry point into writing a book about the subject of intentional living in a way that people can easily relate to and understand.

What This Book Will Teach You

As the subtitle suggests, this book is a real-world approach to living life on your terms.

Within these pages, you'll learn how to:

- Discover what truly matters (Chapter 1: Subject Areas)
- Objectively assess your life (Chapter 2: Progress Reports)
- Identify your highest priorities (Chapter 3: Homework Assignments)
- Organize around your priorities (Chapter 4: Lockers & Backpacks)
- Live proactively instead of reactively (Chapter 5: Study Hall)
- Make the most of your time (Chapter 6: Structured Days)
- Eliminate your major distractions (Chapter 7: Classroom Environments)
- Define clear, meaningful goals (Chapter 8: Majors, Minors & Electives)
- Overcome procrastination (Chapter 9: Lesson Plans)
- Course-correct throughout the year (Chapter 10: Retreats)
- Accelerate your success (Chapter 11: Office Hours)
- Take your learning and growth to a new level (Chapter 12: Extracurricular Activities)

How to Read This Book

I encourage you to read the entire book, cover to cover, before doing any of the assignments at the end of each chapter. Doing so will help you decide if this approach is right for you.

Will it help you at this stage of your life? Is it the right fit based on your unique circumstances? Does it align well with your own personal values and beliefs?

If the answer is "yes," you can find my best recommendation for how to apply this approach in your own life in the conclusion of this book.

Also, you probably noticed that the titles for each chapter are named after specific elements in the formal education system. This was by design, in the hope that the information within these pages will be highly relatable to you, the reader, but please trust that it has nothing to do with *your actual level* of education.

It doesn't matter if you dropped out of high school, it doesn't matter if you earned a college diploma, and it doesn't matter if you pursued an advanced degree in a very specific discipline.

In other words, this approach doesn't discriminate.

It will help you break free from conventional wisdom so you can pursue your own definition of success *regardless* of your formal education experience.

Assuming, of course, you're living in the "real world."

Let's get started.

1

SUBJECT AREAS

DISCOVERING WHAT TRULY MATTERS

"I believe that being successful means having a balance of success stories across the many areas of your life. You can't truly be considered successful in your business life if your home life is in shambles."

— ZIG ZIGLAR

Do you remember how many subjects you were responsible for in school?

In your youth, you may have studied basic subjects like math, science and social studies. You didn't have much of a choice in the matter. These subjects were assigned to you. But as you progressed through the grades, you began to choose which subjects appealed to you the most.

If you wanted to enter the workforce right after high school, you may have chosen to study subjects having to do with the trades. If you wanted to go on to college, you may have chosen subjects that supported your major. The major you selected supported whatever direction you wanted to take your career.

The only difference between school and the real world is this: the stakes are much, much higher in the real world.

In school, if we failed to give a subject area enough attention, it might have resulted in a bad grade on a report card. Certainly not ideal, but not the end of the world either.

In the real world, we no longer need to worry about subject areas; we need to worry about *life areas* instead. Life areas like our health, wealth and relationships. If we fail to pay attention to these areas, we won't get a bad grade. Far worse, it could result in a major catastrophe.

It's up to each and every one of us to discover what these areas are for ourselves. Otherwise, we go on living our lives without an understanding of what truly matters. The problem with this way of living is we might wake up one day to realize we've made compromises in certain areas, compromises of which we were unaware of, and it's too late to go back.

Pre-Determined vs. Custom-Tailored

While I wish I could make a recommendation concerning the areas you should pay attention to and continually balance over time, I can't. I want you to have that certain sense of *ownership* by discovering these areas for yourself.

I've studied dozens of amazing personal development programs over the years. Most programs feature pre-determined life areas like health, career, finances and relationships. While the intention here is good, I walked away from most of those programs feeling like I lacked a sense of ownership.

It was as if I were back in school and the subject areas were being assigned to me again. Why would I study an advanced level of mathematics if I didn't want to become a mathematician? I felt these programs fell a bit short since they didn't take into consideration what mattered most to *me*.

One time, I adopted a program that included "spirituality," but I wasn't interested in that at the time. The suggestion to focus on my spirituality didn't feel right or authentic. In fact, it made me question the integrity of the entire system. I wasted many months trying to adopt an approach that didn't feel congruent with my own personal values and beliefs.

I finally decided to identify which areas of life were relevant to me based on *my* interests. Once I did this, everything changed. Rather than feeling like I was being told what to do, I had a newfound sense of ownership. *I* decided what mattered most based on *my* life.

After recognizing this simple yet powerful distinction, I experienced significant progress in my life in the months that followed.

Identifying Your Areas of Life

The areas of your life demand your constant attention. They require your ongoing effort over the long term. They're directly correlated to your overall well-being and quality of life.

Like the subjects you were responsible for in school, these areas of your life must remain in a constant state of balancing at all times.

This can feel overwhelming *and* empowering at the same time. Overwhelming since you may discover you have so many; empowering since the decision is yours and you get to choose which ones to focus on.

To keep things simple, we'll start by looking at what I call the primary areas of life. These include your health, your wealth and your relationships. These areas can be broken down into multiple subareas, including:

Health

- Spiritual/religious
- Mental/emotional
- Physical

Wealth

- Career/business
- Financial
- Philanthropy

Relationships

- Spouse/partner/significant other
- Children
- Family/friends
- Community/associations/memberships

Take a few moments to identify which areas are relevant for you. If you come up with other areas that aren't included in this list, that's perfectly fine. The goal is to customize these areas based on *where you are in your own life*.

Less is Always More

If you discover seven or more areas of life you may feel a bit overwhelmed.

While it's tempting to identify a lot of areas on your first pass, I've found it helpful to take a *less is more* approach here. I've learned, more times than I'd like to admit, that when everything is important, nothing is important.

That being said, take a few moments to review the list you've come up with. Is there an opportunity to consolidate a few?

I can share my own experience on this. I used to have one specific area for each of my three children. Over time, I found this to be unnecessarily complicated. I've since consolidated these three individual areas into one area called "Children."

Maybe someday it might make sense to split these into three separate areas again, but at this stage of my life, one area is much easier for me to manage.

Arrange in the Order of Importance

Once you've consolidated the areas of your life to the best of your ability, it's time to arrange these areas in the order of importance.

In my life, health is most important. My spiritual, mental/emotional and physical health come before everything else. The reason is simple: if my spirit feels disconnected, if my mind feels turbulent, and if my body feels fatigued, I can't serve those around me at my highest level.

It's like the oxygen mask metaphor. In the event the cabin of an airplane loses pressure mid-flight, you're told to put the mask on yourself *first* before helping those in the seat next to you.

Why?

Because you're of no use to anyone around you when you're stressed out, burned out or passed out.

This is how I've chosen to arrange the areas of my life, but how you arrange yours is completely up to you.

Take a moment to review the areas of your life again and arrange them in the order that feels right to you.

The Constant State of Balancing

In school, you were in a constant state of balancing all the subject areas you were responsible for. You couldn't get away with paying attention to just one subject. If you did, you'd pass one class and fail the rest.

Instead, you studied many subjects at the same time. Throughout the year, you balanced them all to ensure you'd come out ahead in *all* subject areas.

In the real world, the same rules apply. If you pursue your career with a single-pointed focus, you may wake up one day to discover other areas like your health, family or relationships are in jeopardy.

When we go too far outside of balance in one area, we make compromises we may someday regret. If this goes on unchecked for too long, we risk losing *everything*.

In my early and mid-twenties, I wanted one thing: to make lots of money. In fact, my goal was to become a millionaire by the time I turned twenty-five. This was my singular point of focus.

I risked *everything* for this. My mental and physical health were declining, and my relationships were suffering. Ironically enough, the harder I tried to make more money, the more my financial situation got worse.

I was way out of balance, and eventually, I lost my footing and came crashing down. I was lucky to have experienced this at a time in my life when I could afford it, as I didn't have a lot of responsibility back then.

We've all read the headlines about public figures who experience hardships. They have the weight of the world on their shoulders, and they, too, lose their footing from time to time. Often, these hardships include addiction, divorce and, in extreme cases, suicide.

There are many ways to remain in a constant state of balancing, and we'll cover them in greater detail within future chapters.

Remaining Flexible and Open to Change

The areas of your life are never set in stone; they're more like moving targets. They'll change over time based on factors like your current phase of life, interests, responsibilities and desires.

You'll have plenty of opportunities to revisit them in the future.

For now, what's important is that you've identified these areas, consolidated them and arranged them in order of importance.

While subject areas helped us understand what mattered most in school, the areas of our lives help us understand what matters most in the real world.

We'll assess your progress in each area of your life in the next chapter.

Key Points

- While subject areas helped us understand what mattered most in school, the areas of our lives help us understand what matters most in the real world.
- If we fail to pay attention to these areas, we won't get a bad grade. Far worse, it could result in a major catastrophe.

- It's important that you discover these areas for yourself, so you have that certain sense of ownership.
- Less is always more. When everything is important, nothing is important.
- You're of no use to anyone when you're stressed out, burned out or passed out.
- When we go too far outside of balance in one area, we make compromises we may someday regret. If this goes unchecked for too long, we risk losing everything.
- The areas of your life are never set in stone; they're more like moving targets. They'll change over time based on factors like your current phase of life, interests, responsibilities and desires.

Chapter Assignment

1. Identify the areas of your life that matter most.
2. Consolidate these areas to the best of your ability.
3. Arrange these areas in the order of importance.

2

PROGRESS REPORTS
OBJECTIVELY ASSESSING YOUR LIFE

*"What is necessary to change a person is to change his awareness
of himself."*

— ABRAHAM MASLOW

D o you remember getting progress reports in school?

I do. I dreaded the day when progress reports were sent home to my parents. Why? Because these reports told my folks what I already knew: I wasn't doing well in most of the subjects for which I was responsible for.

But these progress reports served an important purpose. They helped us, our teachers and our parents assess how well we were doing (or not doing) in each subject. They provided us with an opportunity to improve our grades before report cards were issued.

In the real world, we're responsible for assessing our own progress as it relates to each area of life. Let's face it: if we don't take charge of this ourselves, who is going to do it for us?

Contrary to what's popular, we shouldn't wait until December 31st to take some inventory. By assessing the areas of your life now, you'll have an instant snapshot of how well you're doing.

Maybe you'll be pleased with the results, or maybe you'll discover you're struggling in certain areas. Either way, awareness is a powerful force. It has a tendency to compel us to make the necessary changes *we know we must make* to improve our lives.

A Better Way to Assess Your Progress

After going bankrupt, I adopted a habit of assessing the areas of my life more frequently. After some time, I started to notice a trend.

Back then, I was rating the areas of my life using a numeric scale from 1-10, where 1 was weak and 10 was strong. I had rated many areas of my life with a score of 7, and I translated this rating as "pretty good."

As I continued on this way for many months, I became more and more comfortable with this rating. It wasn't great, but it felt like I was managing somewhat well for the time being.

One day it dawned on me that a 7 out of 10, when translated into a percentage, equaled 70%. Using a numeric point system became ineffective. After all, if I were still in school, a 70% would translate to a solid "C-." This was like a blow to the gut, and I realized I had once again fallen into the trap of going through the motions in certain areas of my life.

There was, however, a silver lining to this realization. I now understood that using a letter grade was much more objective. Best of all, it created that sense of urgency which helped me make a few necessary changes.

Assigning a Letter Grade

Review the areas of your life that you identified in the previous chapter. Then, assign a letter grade to each area.

I'm referring to the same letter grade system we used in school:

- A (excellent)
- B (good)
- C (fair)
- D (unsatisfactory)
- F (fail)

Don't overthink this, just go with your gut. If you need to, set a timer for twenty seconds and assign whichever grade comes to mind first.

The Gift of Honesty

While assigning a grade to each area, be as honest with yourself as possible. I can't stress the importance of this enough. Honesty is a real gift, and it's one of the most valuable gifts you can give to yourself.

For many years, I assigned a "B" to my physical health area despite the fact that I was severely addicted to tobacco. It never seemed like the "right time" to try yet another attempt at quitting. I dishonestly assigned a letter grade that was by no means objective. I eventually came to terms with my addiction and began assigning an "F" to this area.

This "F" remained for some time, and it certainly discouraged me for a while. It stood out like a sore thumb. Eventually, I could no longer ignore it, and it motivated me enough to make a change. That was the day I realized that with a little extra focus and attention, I could bring that grade back up to a legitimate "B" within a few months. This gave me the perspective I needed, and it compelled me to make what I believe was my *seventh* quit attempt. I'm happy to report that this was the last attempt I would ever have to make.

As the quote at the beginning of this chapter suggests, it's amazing what a little awareness can do for a person. But honesty is always the first step. Having the courage to be honest with yourself gives you an objective and accurate awareness of how well you're doing.

Remember, no one else is looking. Muster up the courage to give yourself the gift of honesty as you assign letter grades to each area of your life.

Calculating the GPA of Your Life

"GPA," short for grade point average, is well-known to many of us as a standard way of measuring achievement. It's used in formal education to calculate your overall grade across *all* subject areas.

We can use a similar formula to measure our progress and achievement in the real world as well.

Once you assign letter grades to each area, you can calculate the GPA of your *life*. To do this, you'll want to assign points to each grade:

- A = 4 points
- B = 3 points
- C = 2 points
- D = 1 point
- F = 0 points

Then, you'll want to add up the total number of points. Once you have the total number of points, divide this number by the total number of areas in your life.

For example, let's say I'm creating a progress report for nine areas of my life, with the following grades and points:

- Spiritual: B (3 points)
- Mental/Emotional: B (3 points)
- Physical: C (2 points)
- Marriage: B (3 points)
- Children: A (4 points)
- Home: C (2 points)
- Family/Friends: B (3 points)
- Mission: B (3 points)
- Wealth: C (2 points)

25 total points / 9 areas of life = 2.77 GPA

Not bad, as we're closing in on a "B" average here.

When I did this for the first time, I was disappointed when I realized I was living a "C" average lifestyle. While I was feeling *comfortable* with my progress, a "C" average felt a bit below my new standards. I had adopted a "C" average identity in school, and I didn't want to relive that same experience in the real world. It compelled me more than ever to improve the GPA of my life to a "B" average or better.

Take a few moments to calculate the GPA of your life. Remember, you're simply looking for that high-level perspective on your overall progress across all areas of your life.

Frequency

When I was in school, progress reports became available at set times throughout the year. However, I recently learned from my

8th grade niece that students can now login to an online portal to see how well they're doing at any time. This is incredibly beneficial!

I've experimented between assessing the areas of my life on a weekly, monthly and quarterly basis. I found monthly and quarterly to be too infrequent, while weekly seems just right. Assessing these areas on a weekly basis helps me to be as proactive as possible with my life.

Ultimately, the frequency in which you assess the areas of your life is completely up to you. I highly encourage you to assess these areas on a weekly basis, at least for a few months. It's like a real-world feedback loop, providing you with the relevant information you need to stay on track. It helps you become more aware of certain issues *early*, giving you a better chance of solving issues *sooner,* so they don't become major problems *later*. You can then reduce the frequency over time if you feel like doing so every week becomes too monotonous.

We'll cover more on *how* to remember to assess these areas of your life every week in a future chapter.

Using a Digital Spreadsheet

After using a journal for many years, I decided to transition to a digital spreadsheet. This made it easier for me to track my progress each week. It also gave me the benefit of being able to review how far I've progressed over specific periods of time.

Here's an example of what this might look like:

	A	H	I	J	K	L	M
1		5/3/XX					
2	Spiritual	B					
3	Mental/Emotional	B					
4	Physical	C					
5	Marriage	B					
6	Children	A					
7	Home	C					
8	Family/Friends	C					
9	Mission	B					
10	Wealth	C					
11	GPA	2.7					

What's also nice about using a digital spreadsheet is that you can "freeze" the first column. This enables you to see historical data while keeping your areas of life in view.

The "Comments" feature is helpful, too. It allows you to add comments that relate back to the grade you've assigned for each specific period:

	A	H	I	J	K	L	M
1		5/3/XX					
2	Spiritual	B					
3	Mental/Emotional	B					
4	Physical	C					
5	Marriage	B					
6	Children	A					
7	Home	C					
8	Family/Friends	C					
9	Mission	B					
10	Wealth	C					
11	GPA	2.7					

Comment on cell H4:
Microsoft Office User
- Get back on track with running regiment 3x/week

Feel free to download the same spreadsheet template I use and customize it to your liking at IntentionalBook.com.

What's important is you're taking the time to assign letter grades to the areas of your life that matter most. How you decide to do it doesn't make much of a difference. A journal will generate the same results as a digital spreadsheet. What you're seeking here is *awareness*.

Sometimes your findings will surprise you, and sometimes they'll disappoint you. Please trust it's a normal reaction. We're in the early stages of our journey here, and we still have a ways to go. All we're looking to do is assess your progress within each area and gain an awareness of how well you're doing (or not doing).

In the next chapter, we'll identify your highest priorities; those that will significantly improve the grades within each area of your life.

Key Points

- In the real world, we're responsible for assessing our own progress as it relates to each area of our life.
- Don't wait until December 31st to take inventory. By assessing the areas of your life now, you'll have an instant snapshot of how well you're doing.
- Awareness is a powerful force. It has a tendency to compel us to make the necessary changes we know we must make to improve our lives.
- Using a letter grade to assess the areas of your life is objective and accurate. It also creates a far greater sense of urgency for you to make some necessary changes.
- Honesty is a real gift, and it's one of the most valuable gifts you can give yourself.
- Calculating the GPA of your life will give you a high-level perspective on your overall progress across all areas of your life.

- Assess the areas of your life on a weekly basis. This will help you become more aware of certain issues early, giving you a better chance of solving issues sooner, so they don't become major problems later.
- Consider using a digital spreadsheet to assess the areas of your life.

~

Chapter Assignment

1. Assess the areas of your life by assigning a letter grade to each one.
2. Calculate the GPA of your life based on the grades you've assigned in the previous step.
3. Use a digital spreadsheet to assess the areas of your life if it makes it easier to track your progress. Feel free to download the same spreadsheet template I use and customize it to your liking at IntentionalBook.com.

3

HOMEWORK ASSIGNMENTS
IDENTIFYING YOUR HIGHEST PRIORITIES

"Things which matter most must never be at the mercy of things which matter least."

— JOHANN WOLFGANG VON GOETHE

R emember how fun and exciting it was to receive homework assignments in school?

Said nobody, ever.

But homework did, in fact, serve three very specific purposes. First, it taught us a lesson in responsibility. Second, it gave us a chance to practice and refine our skills around certain subject areas. Last but not least, it served as another way for us to improve our grades.

In the real world, we're still responsible for homework. Only now, we refer to our homework as our "priorities." As it relates to the many areas of our lives, it's up to us to determine which priorities matter, as well as when we'll focus on them.

There is one exception, and it's in the career or business area of your life. If you work for someone else, you may not have the ability to choose your own priorities. Perhaps they're determined by the person you report to. If this is the case, I believe it's the only exception.

In all other areas of your life, the priorities you choose to focus on will directly impact your grades. When you focus on the right priorities, your grades will improve; when you focus on the wrong ones, your grades will suffer.

Identifying Your Highest Priorities

In the first two chapters, you discovered the areas of your life that mattered most and assigned a letter grade to each one. Now, it's time to brainstorm the many ways you can improve these grades.

Think short-term here, say over the next few weeks. We'll address long-term goals in a future chapter. For now, let's stay focused on the low-hanging fruit.

Imagine you gave yourself a "C" in the physical health area of your life. Would it be possible to bring this grade up to a "C+" or even a "B" in the short term?

When brainstorming ways to improve this grade, your initial list might look like this:

- Reduce the amount of gluten I eat on a daily basis
- Cut out artificial sugars after each meal
- Reduce the amount of caffeine I drink each day
- Throw out all junk food in the pantry
- Exercise 3x a week
- Participate in that fitness class my friend told me about
- Drink 80 ounces of water each day

- Quit my nicotine addiction
- Reduce my alcohol intake on weekends

While this may look like a long and intimidating list, it's a good place to start. And that's all we're going for right now. We'll work toward reducing the feeling of being overwhelmed in a moment.

For now, what's important is that you create a similar list for each area of your life. While doing so, take into consideration the letter grade you assigned to each one. What can you do to "level up" within each area by just one grade?

Reality Check

Remember, we're looking at the short-term here.

In school, it would have been unrealistic to think that you could bring a "D" up to an "A" in a matter of weeks. But it would have been realistic to bring that "D" up to a "D+" or even a "C" in that same time period.

Use this mindset and apply it to your brainstorming.

As you review the list of actions you came up with, be sure they're both realistic *and* doable over the next few weeks.

Again, we'll address long-term goals in a future chapter.

The ONE Thing

Once you've come up with a list of actions you *could* take, review the list, one area at a time, and see if there's *one* action that can improve your grade the most.

This approach was inspired by Gary Keller in his book, *The ONE Thing.*[1] In it, Gary teaches his readers how to find the one thing (or action) that will make everything else easier or unnecessary.

Using the physical health example above, let's say you want to lose some weight this year. While many of the items on that list will assist you with that goal, the one thing you might do over the next few weeks is throw out all the junk food in the pantry. By doing so, you will no longer have convenient access to those late-night snacks. This one step alone could help you lose a few pounds.

This all depends, of course, on your unique situation. If you believe a healthy environment is critical to your success, it's a good choice. If you're on a budget, this won't cost you any money. If you're time-starved, this won't take much time. If you want to do something immediately, you can take this particular action right now.

When choosing the one thing that will improve your grade the most in each area, be sure to consider your unique situation. Again, think realistic *and* doable.

When you identify the one thing, go ahead and circle it. Repeat this step until you have identified the one action that will help you improve your grade the most in each area of your life. Similar to how homework was assigned to you in school, these actions become the *priorities* you'll want to focus on over the next few weeks.

If you're feeling a bit overwhelmed by all the information you've come up with, it's okay. There's no need to do anything with it just yet. Please, simply keep this information in a safe place for now.

We'll cover *how* to effectively organize around all these priorities in the next chapter.

Key Points

- In the real world, we're still responsible for homework. Only now, we refer to our homework as our "priorities."
- As it relates to the areas of our lives, it's up to us to determine which priorities matter and when we'll focus on them.
- The priorities you choose to focus on will directly impact your grades. When you focus on the right priorities, your grades will improve. When you focus on the wrong priorities, your grades will suffer.
- When brainstorming the different ways to improve your grades in each area of your life, be sure those actions are both realistic and doable over the next few weeks.
- It's important to identify the one thing in each area that can help you improve your grade the most.

Chapter Assignment

1. Brainstorm ways to improve your grades within each area of your life.
2. Circle the ONE THING you could do over the next few weeks that will improve your grade the most within each area.

4

LOCKERS & BACKPACKS
ORGANIZING AROUND YOUR PRIORITIES

"Once you have a clear picture of your priorities ... organize around them."

— STEPHEN COVEY

I want to take a moment to congratulate you on all the progress you've made in this journey thus far.

In the first chapter, you learned how to discover the areas of your life that matter most. In the second chapter, you learned how to objectively assess your life by assigning a letter grade to each area. In the third chapter, you learned how to identify your highest priorities.

As you begin reading this chapter, it may feel a bit like your first day of school.

You may experience being overwhelmed due to the new subjects you're responsible for. You're awkwardly trying to carry the weight of all your new textbooks. Homework has already been assigned, and you haven't even made it to your first class!

If this were the case, what's the first thing you'd do?

I bet you'd eagerly search for and find your locker in the hallway. You'd open it and organize all your stuff. You'd fill your backpack with whatever tools you thought were necessary, slam the door and set out to win the day.

If you don't navigate the real world in a similar, organized fashion, the stakes are much higher. In fact, disorganization can negatively impact your health and well-being. Fatigue, stress and higher levels of cortisol are reported by people who feel like their lives are disorganized.[1]

In the real world, it helps to have a "locker" to organize your stuff. This is where you keep all the relevant information pertaining to the areas of your life. It's useful to have a "backpack," too. This is where you keep a suite of tools that will help you become more effective as you set out to win each day.

I'm going to be very frank here: getting organized around your priorities isn't easy, and it's usually not fun, either, but if you stick with it and get this right, the payoff in peace of mind alone will be exponential.

Collecting Dust

I used to be notorious for taking a bunch of important notes and never revisiting them.

While reading a book or taking an online course, I'd fill my notebook with the new material I learned. I would then put that notebook on a shelf, and it would never see the light of day again. The notebook would just sit there collecting dust. I'd stumble on it weeks, months or years later, remember my good intentions, and throw it away.

I don't want this to happen to you.

Eventually, I came to the realization that I didn't have an organizational *system* to support me. My life was a bit of a hot mess, and I would get overwhelmed by all the information I was acquiring. This would cause me to reach a state of paralysis. I moved from one thing to the next, failing to apply whatever I had learned.

As Napoleon Hill suggests in his classic bestseller, *Think and Grow Rich*, "Knowledge is only potential power. It becomes power only when, and if, it is organized into definite plans of action, and directed to a definite end."[2]

If this resonates with you, taking the time to organize around your priorities can make all the difference in the world.

A Simple Solution

Eventually, I came up with a radically simple solution that gives me great peace of mind. I finally have a place to access all the relevant information pertaining to every area of my life, and it's beautifully organized in a practical way that makes sense.

There are *hundreds* of ways to organize around your priorities. Some of the most popular methods include David Allen's *Getting Things Done*,[3] Ryder Carrol's *Bullet Journal*[4] and Tony Robbins's *The Time of Your Life*.[5] I've tried many of the most popular methods, and they're all amazing in their own way.

What I'm about to share with you is, from my perspective, the simplest method to organize around your priorities in the fastest and most effective way possible.

There are two main ideas here, including a "life locker" and a "backpack." While you certainly don't have to follow this exact approach, it's important to solve for both of these main ideas in your own life.

Your "Life Locker"

It's time to decide on what you'll use for your "life locker." This is the place where you'll organize all the relevant information you came up with after completing the assignments in the first three chapters (the areas of your life, the grades you assigned to each area, and the actions you can take to improve each one).

Your life locker can be physical, digital or a combination of both.

I use a combination of both. To solve for my physical storage requirements, I use a simple filing cabinet at home. In it, I have nine folders. Each folder has a tab that represents the nine areas of my life. All the physical documents relevant for each area are organized within each folder.

Now, I appreciate the fact that this may not be enough for *your* unique circumstances. You may have one, two, or three areas in your life that require their own filing cabinet.

If you run a business, you may need a dedicated cabinet for all the relevant files associated with that business. If you're a teacher, you may need a separate cabinet for all your lesson plans and materials. I've had a few clients who have dealt with some major health issues over the years, and they have a separate filing cabinet dedicated to their health histories.

Be sure to take your own physical storage needs into consideration here. What are *your* unique requirements? Take some time to think this through and decide what makes the most sense for your situation.

To solve for my digital requirements, I use a digital storage account (e.g. Dropbox, Google Drive, Box.net). This houses all the relevant digital files pertaining to the many areas of my life.

At the time of this writing, I use a digital storage software called Dropbox. The names of each folder, like the tabs in my filing cabinet, represent each area:

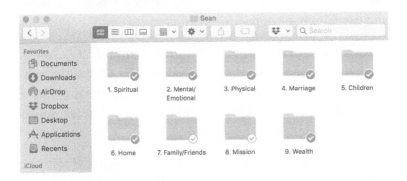

For a video tutorial on how I use Dropbox, please visit IntentionalBook.com.

Once again, be sure to take your own digital storage needs into consideration. What are *your* unique requirements? Of the many available digital storage options, what makes the most sense for you based on your situation?

Once you've made these decisions, it's time to purchase the right tools and set yourself up for success. Take whatever time is necessary to solve for both your physical and digital storage needs. You'll feel a great sense of accomplishment and relief when you're done.

Your "Backpack"

Now it's time to decide what you'll use for your "backpack." This is where you'll keep a suite of tools to help you become more effective as you set out to win each day.

Similar to your life locker, your backpack can be physical, digital or a combination of both.

I use a combination of both here as well. I still use a physical backpack (like the one I used in school). My backpack contains everything I need to win the day: my laptop, Kindle, journal, some writing utensils, a few healthy snacks, a bottle of water and usually a book or two.

Furthermore, I use a project management software (e.g. Asana, Basecamp, Trello). This helps me keep tabs on my projects, priorities and any ideas I've brainstormed along the way. I have instant access to all this relevant information online, as well as via an app installed on my smartphone.

At the time of this writing, I use a project management software called Asana. It's like a glorified to-do list, and it appeals to me because of its simplicity.

Within my Asana account, I use the "projects" feature to represent the areas of my life:

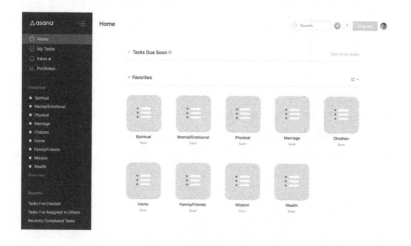

Then, within each area of my life, I've created three sections to help me organize all the relevant information:

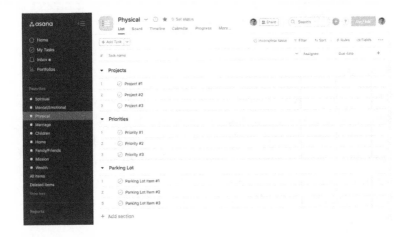

Projects

This section includes active projects I'm currently working on. I define a project as an action that requires more than one step, and more than two weeks of my focus, to complete. This is unlike a "to-do," which may only take a few minutes to a few hours.

Remember the assignment from the last chapter? You circled the one thing in each area of your life that could improve your grade the most. Do any of these actions contain more than one step or require more than two weeks of your focus to complete? If so, you may want to consider these actions as "projects" instead.

This may eliminate those unpleasant surprises when you realize what you thought was a to-do actually takes much longer than you initially anticipated.

I value project management software because it allows me to easily break my projects down into manageable steps. But you can also do this in a notebook. We'll cover more on *how* to break your projects down into manageable steps in a future chapter.

For now, simply consider the importance of recognizing a project when you see one.

Priorities

This section includes any actions that are relevant for the coming days, weeks and months ahead. I define a priority as a to-do that takes anywhere from a few minutes to a few hours to complete. This is unlike a project, which may require more than one step and more than two weeks of my focus. Once I assign a specific due date to an action it becomes a priority in my life.

Are any of the actions you circled in the assignment from the last chapter more of a to-do vs. a project? If so, you might want to assign a due date to it and consider it a *priority*.

Using the physical health example from the last chapter, we referenced throwing out the junk food in the pantry. This probably isn't a project. It's more of a to-do as it should take less than an hour to complete. Unless, of course, you have an unusually large pantry. Assuming that's not the case, you should assign a due date to it and consider it a priority.

You may find that some of your priorities are *recurring* priorities; they happen more than once. Actions like filling the water softener, changing the furnace filter and getting a haircut every few weeks are good examples of recurring priorities.

Here's a unique example. Every Tuesday, I write my wife an email thanking her for everything she has done for me over the past week. On Sundays, I review my gratitude journal and put an asterisk next to all the entries describing how she has contributed to my life. Like clockwork, when Tuesday rolls around, I send this email letting her know how much I appreciate her efforts.

This is another reason I value project management software. I'm able to effortlessly complete these types of recurring priorities because the software reminds me. They're set to recur, and once completed, the software automatically creates another priority for the following period.

I also find this feature helpful for birthdays and holidays. I used to scramble to pick up cards, flowers and gifts for loved ones at the last minute. Now, my project management software reminds me well in advance. As a result, I feel more proactive about some of the more important occasions in my life.

Again, it doesn't matter if you use project management software or a notebook. For now, simply consider the importance of recognizing the priorities in your life and planning to focus on them accordingly.

Parking Lot

This section includes any actions that may be relevant in the future. The parking lot doesn't have to be limited to just actions, either. What you capture here can include ideas, issues, opportunities and future projects. Anything you don't want to lose sight of can be captured here.

For all the actions you didn't circle from the assignment in the last chapter, consider capturing them in the "parking lot" section within each area of your life. This way, you'll have the benefit of being able to reference them at a later time.

I recently overheard my wife talking to a friend who had just enrolled in a series of cooking classes. My wife was really excited about this idea, so I added it to the parking lot section within the "Marriage" area of my life. I have peace of mind for two reasons: I have a great gift idea for the next occasion, and since I've captured it, I have certainty that I'll remember it.

Did you know it's estimated that we have *sixty to eighty thousand thoughts* a day?[6] What's really scary is that many of these thoughts are repeat offenders. They're the same thoughts we had yesterday, last week and last year! The parking lot section gives us a place to capture our thoughts and ideas in real time.

By capturing these thoughts in the parking lot section within each area of our life, we free up some much-needed bandwidth. We can then reallocate this bandwidth for creative thinking and problem solving.

At the risk of sounding like I'm trying to convince you, this is yet another reason I value project management software. It gives me great peace of mind to know that, at any given time, I can capture an idea and organize it properly. I can do this from my laptop or from the app on my smartphone when I'm on the go.

For a video tutorial on how I use Asana, please visit IntentionalBook.com.

Once again, you can use a project management software or a notebook. What matters is that you consider the importance of proactively capturing your ideas so you can easily reference them later.

It's time to determine what you'll use for your "backpack." What are *your* unique requirements?

Maybe it's a physical item, a suite of digital tools or a combination of both. Take some time to think this through and decide what makes the most sense based on your situation.

Once you've made these decisions, you can purchase the right suite of tools and become more effective as you set out to win each day.

Don't Rush This

Before reading any further, be sure to carve out whatever time you need to organize around your highest priorities. Take the necessary time to organize all the relevant information you came up with in the first three chapters, solving for both your physical and digital storage needs along the way.

This may seem like a boring, frustrating and even overwhelming undertaking, but it's an important one. By carefully following the instructions in this chapter, you'll be organizing around your priorities in the fastest and most effective way possible.

Get this right, and the next chapter on living proactively will complement your efforts beautifully.

Key Points

- Being disorganized can negatively impact your overall health and well-being.
- Getting organized around your priorities isn't easy, and it's usually not fun, either, but the payoff in peace of mind alone will be exponential.
- It helps to have a "life locker." This is the place where you organize all the information pertaining to the many areas of your life.
- It also helps to use a "backpack." This is where you'll keep a suite of tools that helps you become more effective so you can set out to win each day.
- You can organize all the actions in your life into three distinct categories: projects, priorities and parking lot.
- It doesn't matter if you use physical or digital tools to get organized. What matters is you organize around

your priorities in a way that makes the most sense
for you.

Chapter Assignment

1. Based on your own unique requirements, decide what
   you'll use for your "life locker" and your "backpack."
   For video tutorials on how I use Dropbox and Asana,
   please visit IntentionalBook.com.
2. Purchase these appropriate tools.
3. Invest as much time as necessary to capture the
   information you came up with in the first three
   chapters and organize around your priorities.

5

STUDY HALL

LIVING PROACTIVELY INSTEAD OF REACTIVELY

"If you're proactive, you focus on preparing. If you're reactive, you end up focusing on repairing."

— JOHN C. MAXWELL

Do you remember what it was like to sit through study hall period?

For some students, this was a time to catch up, reset and prepare for the rest of the week. For me, this was a time to catch up on my sleep.

The room where I attended study hall was large enough that I could blend into the crowd. If I got there early enough, I could claim a desk in the back row. I would place an open book on the desk, support my head with my hand, and shield my eyes so the teacher assumed I was studying.

Worked like a charm.

While I didn't use my time in study hall very wisely, I do recall many of my peers taking it more seriously. Those who did take it seriously performed well in school.

Study hall serves a very important purpose. It gives students an opportunity to be more *proactive* with their efforts.

If, like me, you didn't take advantage of this downtime, you may have felt a little *reactive* with your efforts. I remember being in a constant state of worry. Impending due dates involving home-work, quizzes and tests usually got the best of me. It was an incredibly stressful way to navigate school, and I've come to realize it was completely *unnecessary* for me to experience all that stress.

In the real world, it's not easy to carve out the time from our busy schedules to catch up, reset and prepare for the week ahead. But if we don't set aside some time, we'll experience the same stress we experienced in school: conflicts in our schedule, failing to prepare for commitments we've made, missed dead-lines and scrambling to catch up when we've fallen behind.

It's more of the same stress, but on a much larger scale.

When we do take the time to prepare our week in advance, we transition from what feels like a *reactive* life to a more *proactive* one.

The Benefits of Being Proactive

I used to be very reactive as I entered each week. On Monday, I wouldn't know what events were scheduled in the days ahead, what commitments I had already made, or how much free time I had. I didn't even know which priorities I should focus on. Instead, I tackled what I believed were priorities, to the best of my ability, as they came screaming in my direction.

It felt like I was shooting everything in the bushes that moved.

I began taking a small amount of time on Sunday afternoon to prepare my week in advance. I'm not referring to creating a detailed plan for the week, as we both know it's impossible to predict what will happen too far in advance. I'm referring to reviewing the coming week from more of a high-level perspective.

After doing this for a few weeks, I was very pleased with the results. Conflicts decreased. I felt more prepared for pre-existing commitments. Key priorities I wanted to focus on were identified and actually completed for once.

I no longer felt like I was reacting to everyone and everything else. Instead, it felt like I was living more proactively than ever before.

After many years of trial and error, I came up with a simple agenda that helps me stay focused as I review the coming week. I hope you'll take it into serious consideration, experience the benefits for yourself, and then customize it to your liking.

The Weekly Review

First, you'll need to find a time in your schedule where you can invest about thirty minutes to review the week ahead. If that seems like a lot, consider what Brian Tracy has to say about investing time to plan in his book, *Master Your Time, Master Your Life*:

"Every minute that you spend planning your work will save you at least 10 minutes in getting your work done . . . That is more than a 1,000 percent return on your energy."[1]

I've found this to be true in my own life, and I hope you'll take Brian's guidance seriously here and find it to be true in yours, too.

I usually perform my weekly review on Sunday afternoons, but I'll perform it on Monday mornings when my Sundays are jam-packed with family activities. It doesn't matter what day and time you choose to do your weekly review. Wherever you can find a small window in your schedule will work just fine.

Next, you'll want to block out the time in your planner or calendar. This will remind you that you've made a commitment with yourself to review your week in advance.

If you use a digital calendar, set this block of time to repeat forever. Don't worry, I'm only encouraging you to try this *once*. When you experience the results, the notion of *forever* won't seem like such a scary thing.

Sample Agenda

Here's a sample agenda for your consideration:

What: The Weekly Review

When: Sundays @ 4pm

Where: My Favorite Coffee Shop

1. Assess the Areas of Your Life (5 minutes)
2. Review Calendar for the Coming Week (5 minutes)
3. Benchmark Projects & Identify Steps (10 minutes)
4. Identify Priorities & Assign Due Dates (10 minutes)

In this example, it'll take thirty minutes to perform the weekly review.

For clarification purposes, let's review each item on this sample agenda.

Assess the Areas of Your Life

This helps you get a quick pulse on how well you're doing in every area of your life. Assign a letter grade to each area and calculate your updated GPA. If you discover a certain area to be significantly off-track, consider which actions you can take in the coming week to improve your grade. Make a note of these actions and recognize them as *priorities* you'll want to focus on over the next seven days.

Review Calendar for the Coming Week

This helps you get a head-start on your week. While reviewing your calendar, you may find a few conflicts in your schedule. Now is the time to be proactive and resolve these conflicts well in advance. You might also notice an existing commitment, like a phone call or a meeting, that you need to prepare for. Make a note and recognize either of these occurrences as more priorities you'll want to focus on in the coming week.

Benchmark Projects & Identify Steps

This helps you course-correct your projects. Here's where you'll check in on your existing projects to make sure they're still on track. Are the steps that support your projects still accurate and in the right order? If not, you can take some time to adjust your course before it's too late. If your steps are accurate and in the right order, now is the time to identify the steps you'll focus on in the coming week. Make a note and recognize these steps as more priorities you'll want to focus on over the next seven days. We'll cover more on identifying projects that support your goals and breaking them down into manageable steps in a later chapter.

Identify Priorities & Assign Due Dates

This helps you identify the priorities you'll want to focus on over the next week. Here's where you'll review the areas of your life and decide which priorities will get your attention. Then, you'll assign due dates for each priority, spreading them out evenly over the next seven days. By doing this, you'll have a better awareness for your time capacity each day.

Feel free to download the same weekly review agenda I use and customize it to your liking at IntentionalBook.com.

Adding the Agenda to Your Digital Calendar

I like to add this agenda to the notes section in my digital calendar to act as a reminder of what I'm supposed to do when performing my weekly review:

Using a Carrot

If you find it difficult to commit to performing the weekly review, try using a "carrot." This is an item you can place at the beginning of your agenda that will compel you to take action.

Author and habit expert James Clear refers to this strategy as "temptation bundling." In his book *Atomic Habits*, he states, "We need to make our habits attractive because it is the expectation of a rewarding experience that motivates us to act in the first place. This is where a strategy known as temptation bundling comes into play." He goes on to say, "Temptation bundling works by linking an action you want to do with an action you need to do."[2]

Once you're in the rhythm of performing the weekly review, I'll make a bold prediction that you'll never skip it again, but the first time can be the most difficult.

Before this became a positive habit in my life, I constantly blew off these meetings with myself. My intentions were good. I even blocked it out on my calendar. But when the time came, I failed to follow through.

Who knew that being accountable to yourself could be so difficult?

I added thirty minutes of reading to the beginning of the agenda, and this did the trick since I'm passionate about learning. After reading for thirty minutes, my eyes typically need a break. I found this to be the perfect time to transition into the balance of the agenda.

What sort of a "carrot" could you use to compel you to perform your weekly review? Could you read a book? Meditate for ten minutes? Listen to your favorite podcast? Watch some videos online? Browse your favorite social media platform?

The options are endless.

Using a Timer

I recently began using a timer for each item on the agenda. There is something about "beating the buzzer" that appeals to me, and it helps me stay focused. I simply load up the minutes on the clock app installed on my smartphone, start the timer, and away I go.

When I begin my weekly review, I set my timer for thirty minutes and read. Next, I reset the timer for five minutes while I review my calendar. Then, I reset the timer for ten minutes while I review my projects and steps. Finally, I reset it for another ten minutes while I decide which priorities I'll focus on for the coming week and assign due dates to each one.

I'm usually done with each item on my agenda before the timer goes off, but I do get distracted on occasion. When I go down a rabbit hole, the buzzer helps me refocus my attention on completing the next item on the agenda.

Are you easily distracted? If so, try using a timer to help you stay focused.

Long-Term Planning

In addition to the weekly review, there are two agendas I'll ask you to consider in a later chapter. These agendas will help you course-correct more effectively throughout the year:

- The Quarterly Retreat
- The Annual Retreat

For now, take a few minutes to create your own weekly review agenda. Then, identify a day and time in your schedule where you can commit to it.

Reviewing your week in advance can become a powerful habit. Like study hall, doing so helps you catch up, reset and prepare for the week ahead. You'll feel like you're living more proactively than ever before after performing your first weekly review.

In the next chapter, we'll cover a simple yet effective way to make the most of each day as you enter your week.

Key Points

- When we do take the time to prepare our week in advance, we transition from what feels like a *reactive* life to a more *proactive* one.
- "Every minute that you spend planning your work will save you at least 10 minutes in getting your work done . . . That is more than a 1,000 percent return on your energy."
- If you find it difficult to commit to performing the weekly review, try using a "carrot." This is an item you can place at the beginning of your agenda that will compel you to take action.
- If you're easily distracted, try using a timer during your weekly review to help you stay focused.
- Reviewing your week in advance can become a powerful habit; doing so helps you catch up, reset and prepare for the week ahead.

Chapter Assignment

1. Create your own weekly review agenda. Feel free to download my customizable template at IntentionalBook.com.
2. Decide which day and time you'll commit to performing it.
3. Block out this day and time in your planner or calendar (if you use a digital calendar, schedule a recurring block that repeats forever).
4. Perform the weekly review once in the coming week and pay close attention to the results you experience.

6

STRUCTURED DAYS
MAKING THE MOST OF YOUR TIME

"It's hard to be fully creative without structure and constraint. Try to paint without a canvas. Creativity and freedom are two sides of the same coin."

— DAVID ALLEN

In school, my days were incredibly structured. I got settled in to my first period (algebra–yikes), and before I knew it the bell would ring. I'd pack up my things and scramble to my next class. This pattern repeated itself for what felt like the longest days of my life. Eventually, the last bell rang, and school was finally out.

Thank goodness.

I don't know about you, but this rigid structure bored me to tears. So much so that my friends and I would often cut the class right after lunch. Luckily for us, we knew the students who walked the halls and took the attendance slips from the teachers. These students would manipulate the slips before handing them into the principal's office. My friends and I would head to the empty gym and play *badminton* of all things just to get some much-needed variety into our schedules.

In hindsight, this structure did, in fact, serve an important purpose. Students are responsible for studying many subject areas all at once. Teachers are responsible for teaching these subjects as effectively as possible. There's a lot of ground to cover, both from the students' perspectives, as well as the teachers'. Structure acts as the glue that holds everything in place. It keeps everyone on pace each day to achieve specific outcomes throughout the school year.

In the real world, we risk being *ineffective* when we fail to maintain a certain degree of structure in our lives. I believe it's up to us to determine the best way to structure our days so we can make the most of our time. This applies as much to stay-at-home parents as it does to career-driven professionals.

I don't know about you, but I'm not interested in being ineffective. I want to be as effective as possible with the time I'm blessed with every day. I view each day like a disintegrating gift; once today becomes yesterday, it's in the history books and I'll never get it back.

Freedom in Structure

Contrary to what some of us experienced in school, structure can be a *good* thing.

Sure, structure can keep us on track to achieve our priorities for the day. When our daily priorities are on track, our priorities for the week remain on track, and when our weekly priorities are on track, our priorities for the month are on track.

You get the idea.

What's counterintuitive about applying structure to our day is that we can actually find more *freedom* in it.

For many years, I didn't understand this. I thought structure was too "rigid" for my lifestyle. I avoided structure like the plague, even though my role models were encouraging me to add it to my daily routine.

After experiencing weeks' worth of frustration because I wasn't making any progress on an important project, I finally decided to add a bit of structure to my day. I worked my way through the resistance and took a few minutes to block time in my schedule. To my surprise, I didn't suffocate to death. In fact, I was shocked when I looked back at the results that evening.

Never in my life had I experienced such an effective day.

Projects finally got the attention they deserved. Priorities got taken care of at the right time, in the right order. Transitioning from one activity to the next became effortless. To my surprise, I had more time throughout the day than I originally anticipated.

When evening rolled around, I had four hours of uninterrupted time with my family. Not only was I physically present, but I was mentally present, too. I had made the most of my time that day, and there was nothing left to do but appreciate the people in my life who mattered most.

It was an empowering feeling. I thought if I could replicate my efforts the next day, it would be an amazing week, and I was right.

The Compound Effect

I first learned the penny lesson from Darren Hardy in his book, *The Compound Effect*.[1] Here's the gist of it:

Imagine you are given two options. You can have three million dollars today, or a penny doubled every day for thirty-one days. Which one would you choose?

Three million dollars today is awfully tempting, but if you choose a penny doubled every day for thirty-one days, you would have over *ten million* dollars.

You can take advantage of the compound effect as it pertains to *your time* each day.

Imagine adding some structure to your day. Then, imagine honoring that structure for weeks at a time. The power of the compound effect will directly apply to the progress you're making in every area of your life.

For instance, let's apply the compound effect to the GPA of your life. Say you started with a 2.5 GPA. What if all you did was make a *one percent* change each week? That 2.5 GPA becomes a 2.53 the following week. Nothing special, right? But wait. Keep going. If you kept improving by just one percent every week, you'll be looking at a 4.0 within the next twelve months.

While achieving a GPA of 4.0 in your life may never be possible, you get the idea.

Think about it. Days compound into weeks. Weeks compound into months. Months compound into quarters. Quarters compound into *years*.

Adding some structure to your day can significantly alter the trajectory of your future.

The Daily Plan

Similar to the weekly review, I've come up with what I call the "daily plan." I hope you'll take this into serious consideration, too, and experience the benefits for yourself.

First, you'll need to find a time in your schedule where you can invest about fifteen minutes to plan your day. I prefer to do this in the morning, before my day begins. Some of the clients I've taught prefer to do this in the evening prior to the following day. Wherever you can find time in your schedule will do.

Next, you'll want to block out the time in your planner or calendar. This will remind you that you've made a commitment to yourself to plan your day.

If you use a digital calendar, set this fifteen-minute block of time to repeat forever. Like the weekly review, I only encourage you to try this *once* and experience the results for yourself.

Sample Agenda

For your consideration, here's a sample agenda you can follow:

What: The Daily Plan

When: Monday - Friday @ 8am

Where: Home Office

1. Review Calendar for the Day (5 minutes)
2. Identify Priorities for the Day (5 minutes)
3. Schedule Priorities in Calendar (5 minutes)

In this example, it'll only take fifteen minutes to perform the daily plan.

For clarification purposes, let's review each item on this sample agenda.

Review Calendar for the Day

This helps you review your day in advance to gauge how much "white space" you'll have throughout the day. If you catch a last-minute conflict, now's a good time to resolve it. You may even notice an existing commitment, like a phone call or a meeting, that you need to prepare for. When this is the case, make a note of it and treat it as a new priority for the day.

Identify Priorities for the Day

Assuming you performed the weekly review, you should already have your priorities identified, but we all know things can change. This gives you a chance to make sure the priorities you identified during your weekly review are still relevant. This also serves as a good opportunity to identify any new priorities you'd like to focus on for the day.

Schedule Priorities in Calendar

Now you schedule the priorities you've identified into your calendar. This helps you get a more accurate sense of how long your priorities will actually take. It also helps you to realistically understand your time capacity in a given day. Once your priorities are scheduled in your calendar, it's a matter of entering your day and hitting your marks.

Feel free to download the same daily plan agenda I use and make it your own at IntentionalBook.com.

Adding the Agenda to Your Digital Calendar

Like the weekly review, I like to add the daily plan agenda to the notes section in my digital calendar. This acts as a reminder of what I'm supposed to do when performing my daily plan.

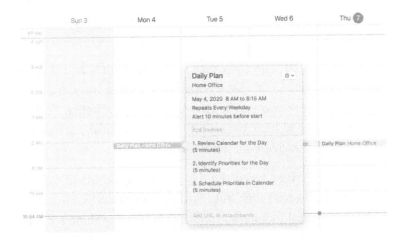

Using a Carrot and a Timer

If you're finding the daily plan difficult to commit to, feel free to add a carrot to the beginning of the agenda. What sort of "carrot" might you use to compel you to take action?

Also, if you find yourself getting distracted while performing your daily plan, try using a timer to help you stay focused.

Triage

It's important to get good at triaging when things don't go as planned (and believe me, this will be often). Most days you'll get interrupted, distracted and pulled in all sorts of directions. Your ability to get right back into your calendar is critical. Learning to triage will help you refocus your energies for the balance of the day.

Here is a real-time example: this morning, I scheduled a three-hour block for writing this very chapter. About an hour into it my wife called with an emergency (she's the only contact in my phone with emergency bypass access, something we'll cover in the next chapter). I had to save my progress, travel back home and be with my daughter while she took my youngest son to the doctor.

Before I learned how to triage my calendar, I would have become frustrated and angry when my morning was derailed. I would have been short with my wife when I got home. Feeling defeated, I would have blown off the balance of my afternoon and invested it instead on mindless distractions.

My ability to triage saved the day. No, my good intentions for the morning weren't met, but I had peace of mind knowing I'd be back to my calendar after lunch. This *knowing* alone reduced my stress and frustration when a sudden change of plans interrupted my schedule. After moving some things around, I'm back to focusing on my writing priority for the day.

You *must* remain flexible when scheduling your day. Interruptions and distractions will happen. Expect lots of them. When they do happen (and they will), remember to be patient and compassionate with yourself as well as others.

Triaging is an artform that takes time and practice to get the hang of and improve upon. When you plan your day for the first time, expect to triage your calendar at least once. Look at the many distractions and interruptions you'll inevitably face as blessings in disguise. They unexpectedly show up to help you improve your ability to triage and roll with the punches.

Eighty Percent Compliance

Nobody is 100 percent in control of what happens throughout his or her day. Those who think they are often set themselves up for frustration and disappointment.

I encourage you to strive for *80 percent compliance* here. As long as you hit your marks to the tune of 80 percent on the days you add structure, you'll be in great shape toward the end of the week.

When things outside your control do interrupt your schedule, remember to breathe. Have peace of mind knowing you can practice the art of triaging the moment you're back to your calendar.

Travel Time

Have you ever been in a rush to make a meeting or an appointment on time? We've all been there, and it's no fun. By scheduling your travel time, you'll be far less likely to experience the stress of rushing out the door because you're running late.

I've developed the habit of scheduling travel time in my calendar in fifteen-minute increments, even if I'm only traveling five. When it comes to making appointments on time, I no longer have to worry about traffic conditions and all sorts of other unknowns.

If this resonates with you, consider adding blocks in your schedule for travel time.

Family Time

This one's my favorite.

I used to think family time would just happen on its own. The truth is it doesn't. Family time slips by like everything else if I'm not more intentional about it.

Monday through Friday, there is a block in my calendar called "Family Time" between 5:30 p.m. and 8:30 p.m. This acts as a reminder to give myself permission to tune everything else out. I do my best to be fully present with my wife and children. The only concern I have during this time is to be fully present with the ones I love.

If this resonates with you, consider adding blocks in your schedule for family time.

Movies, Sports, Entertainment

It may seem strange, but my wife and I have gotten into the habit of scheduling our entertainment. Movies, sports and musicals are scheduled on our shared calendar. This gives us something exciting to look forward to and it serves as a good reminder to be fully present with one another.

Even when we're planning on watching a movie at home, we'll schedule it. We make popcorn and drinks, snuggle up on the couch, and enjoy each other's company (as well as the movie). Our smartphones are in another room, and we're fully present with the activity at hand.

If this resonates with you, consider adding blocks in your schedule for things like movies, sports and other forms of entertainment.

Weekends Optional

You'll have to decide when and where you'll introduce structure in your schedule.

For me, having structure Monday through Friday helps me make the most of my time during my "work week." I leave my weekends to chance as I look forward to the spontaneous nature of what Saturdays and Sundays will bring.

I value both structure *and* variety, so this is the combination that works best for me. I encourage you to decide what type of structure works best for you based on *your own* existing circumstances.

Extra Credit: Morning and Evening Routines

You may want to consider adding a reoccurring block of time in the morning or in the evening (or both) for *routines*.

I begin every day with a very simple routine. There's a block in my calendar called "Morning Routine" from 5:30 a.m. to 6:15 a.m. It consists of gratitude journaling, exercising or stretching, drinking a glass of water and getting ready for the day.

In the evening, I like to wind down in an effort to maximize my sleep efficiency. There's a block in my calendar called "Evening Routine" from 8:30 p.m. to 9:15 p.m. This routine consists of getting ready for bed, more gratitude journaling and some light reading.

Please consider whether these morning or evening routines would benefit you. If so, you can come up with your own micro-agenda and add these blocks to your calendar as reminders of how you'd like to intentionally begin and end each day.

Sample Screenshot

If you're curious, here's a sample screenshot of what a typical workweek might look like on my calendar.

Every time I share my calendar with my clients, they think I'm crazy, but I've seen them change their minds after just one day of adding structure to their own schedules.

Consider Stephen Covey's perspective on this in *The 7 Habits of Highly Effective People*. "The key is not to prioritize what's on your schedule, but to schedule your priorities."[2]

In the next chapter, we'll learn how to be more protective of our time by eliminating the major distractions we face on a daily basis so we can stay laser-focused on our highest priorities.

Key Points

- In the real world, we risk being ineffective when we fail to maintain a certain degree of structure in our lives.
- Structure can keep us on track to achieve our priorities for the day while at the same time providing us with a certain degree of freedom.
- Thanks to the compound effect, adding structure to your day can significantly alter the trajectory of your future.

- If you're finding the daily plan difficult to commit to, feel free to add a carrot to the beginning of the agenda.
- If you find yourself getting distracted while performing your daily plan, try using a timer to help you stay focused.
- It's important to get good at triaging when things don't go as planned (which will be often).
- You must remain flexible when scheduling your day. Remember to be patient and compassionate with yourself as well as others.
- Strive for 80 percent compliance. As long as you hit your marks to the tune of 80 percent each day, you'll be in great shape toward the end of the week.
- Consider adding travel time, family time, sports, movies and entertainment to your schedule.
- To become more intentional about how you begin and end each day, consider adopting a morning and evening routine.

∼

Chapter Assignment

1. Create your own daily plan agenda. You can download my template and make it your own at IntentionalBook.com.
2. Decide which days and times you'll commit to performing it.
3. Mark these days and times in your planner or calendar (if you use a digital calendar, schedule a recurring block that repeats forever).
4. Perform the daily plan as soon as possible, and pay close attention to the results you experience.

7

CLASSROOM ENVIRONMENTS
ELIMINATING YOUR MAJOR DISTRACTIONS

"You are the master of your destiny. You can influence, direct and control your own environment. You can make your life what you want it to be."

— NAPOLEON HILL

L et's pause for a moment to appreciate all the progress you've made in your journey thus far.

In the fourth chapter, you learned how to organize around your highest priorities. In the fifth chapter, you learned how to live proactively instead of reactively by performing the weekly review. In the sixth chapter, you learned how to make the most of your time by performing the daily plan and adding structure to your day.

Despite all this progress, you may still find yourself getting pulled in all sorts of directions. To understand *why*, let's think back to what it was like to sit in a typical classroom.

There was a focal point in the room, usually in the front, where the teacher would teach. Students sat opposite the teacher. No unnecessary technology was being used. The general decor of the room related back to whatever subject was being taught.

Classrooms create a focus-rich environment that is conducive to the students' success.

It has become increasingly difficult to recreate that same focus-rich environment in the real world. Unless we take the time to safeguard our attention, we face an endless sea of distraction that can constantly hijack our ability to focus.

Are you treating your daily environment like a virtual class-room and safeguarding your focus? Or are you allowing distractions to run rampant throughout your day?

The Bad News

We live in the Information Age, and while it brings with it many benefits, it also brings with it many disadvantages, too.

Most of us are exposed to hundreds, if not thousands, of marketing messages every day. Furthermore, recent reports suggest that the average U.S. adult spends just under *four hours* per day on their mobile device.[1]

We carry these weapons of mass distraction with us every-where we go. Our smartphones incessantly vibrate, beep and ring. If we don't take protective measures, these devices will continue diverting our attention away from the present moment.

The Attention Rush

In the nineteenth century, many people moved in droves to California in search of great fortune. This period was known as *The Gold Rush* of the late 1840's.

I predict that the period we're living in will one day be known as *The Attention Rush* of the twenty-first century. Everyone is competing for our attention, and so is every business. I believe our attention is the number one asset we have as human beings. It's up to each and every one of us to protect our attention like it's gold, *because it is.*

Unfortunately, many of us tend to give away our attention like it's a worthless commodity. We place our attention on whatever seems to be interesting at any given moment. It's important to break this habit and start appreciating the *power* of our attention. By doing so, we'll begin to value our attention for what it's truly worth.

The Good News

With a little effort, we *can* control many of the things that distract us in our daily environment.

Years ago, my email inbox was the worst offender. I was bombarded all day long with new emails from friends, family, clients and the many subscriptions I had signed up for (and some I hadn't). I was drowning in a windfall of new messages every single day. I simply couldn't keep up with it all.

When I finally became aware of my problem, I tried to solve it. I started by turning off the audible notification whenever a new email arrived in my inbox. This worked for a while, but over time I formed a new habit: I would scroll over the task bar on my laptop to see if there were any new notifications waiting for me.

You know that icon, the one with the small little circle containing a number inside? It can be quite enticing! The temptation was too hard to resist, and I always gave in, checking to see what was waiting for me in my inbox.

I then learned how to change my email setting to "pull" instead of "push" (the default setting on most devices). This way, new messages would only arrive in my inbox on my command. The "pull" setting helped for some time until I noticed messages were still being pushed to my inbox even when I wasn't asking for them!

I finally decided to take a full-measure approach: I shut down my email program entirely.

Now, if I'm not reading or writing emails, my email program isn't open on my laptop or smartphone. This completely eliminates any risk associated with distractions. It has also freed up what I would imagine equates to days' worth of my time and attention. I've since reinvested this time into the people and the priorities that matter most in my life.

Do certain parts of this story resonate with you?

Your Worst Offender

What's *your* worst offender?

Is it binging on the latest Netflix series? Scrolling endlessly through your favorite social media feed? Getting sucked into one recommended video after the next on YouTube? Clicking around aimlessly on your smartphone?

I'm not judging, by the way. I've struggled with them all.

Let's say your worst offender is your smartphone, and your intention is to spend less of your precious time on it. There are a host of actions you could take to eliminate this distraction.

For starters, gaining an awareness of how much time you spend on your smartphone is key. Most smartphones provide a report of how much time you're spending on your screen. This report is usually found in the settings area. It can give you a sobering look into how much of your attention that little device demands.

If you're not familiar with the screen time report, a quick Google search will show you exactly how to find it.

Here's an example of what this report looks like on my smartphone:

While averaging two hours per day may not seem so bad, doing the math suggests otherwise.

If you average two hours a day like I do, multiply this by 365 days a year. Then multiply this number by the number of years you assume you'll be alive. Divide that number by twenty-four hours in a day, and you get a sense of how many days you'll spend on your smartphone.

Taking it a step further, you can divide again by 365 days in a year. This will give you a sense of how many *years* you'll be spending on your smartphone if you decide to keep the status quo.

Here's how this would play out in my own life:

2 hours per day x 365 days a year = 730 hours per year.

730 hours per year x 50 more years I hope to be alive = 36,500 hours.

36,500 hours of screen time / 24 hours in a day = 1,521 days.

1,521 days / 365 days per year = 4.16 years.

At this pace, I'll spend over *four years of my life* staring at the screen of my smartphone.

Imagine what you could do if you took back four entire years of your life! This is an amazing exercise. If you're distracted by your smartphone, I encourage you to take the time to do the math for yourself.

I recently watched *Wall-E* with my six-year-old son. During the second half of the movie, there was a scene where the power went out on the spaceship. Those who had been doing nothing but watching a screen suddenly snapped out of their hypnosis. They were dazed and confused, not knowing exactly where they were or how they got there.

Is it possible that the writers of *Wall-E* were hinting at the current state of affairs in the real world?

Quieting the Noise

The screen time report also provides you with a breakdown of which apps you use the most and which ones you use the least.

For a quick win, you can delete the apps you rarely use. Then, you could adjust the settings within the apps you use the most. Turning off the audible notification when new alerts or messages arrive is a good start. You can even disable the tiny icon that appears next to your apps when there are new, unread alerts or messages.

Sound scary? You bet it is.

Here's the thing: most of us underestimate the ferociousness of this opponent. There's an actual science behind why these incoming messages are so compelling.

As Daniel J. Levitin writes in his book, *The Organized Mind: Thinking Straight in the Age of Information Overload*, "Text messages magically appear on the screen of your phone and demand immediate attention from you. Add to that the social expectation that an unanswered text feels insulting to the sender, and you've got a recipe for addiction: You receive a text, and that activates your novelty centers. You respond and feel rewarded for having completed a task (even though that task was entirely unknown to you fifteen seconds earlier). Each of those delivers a shot of dopamine as your limbic system cries out "More! More! Give me more!"[2]

In true full-measure form, I've also been experimenting with the "Do Not Disturb" feature on my smartphone. So far, I'm thrilled with the results. All incoming noise, both auditory and visual, is silenced when using this feature. There is one exception, and it's my wife. She's the only contact in my phone with "emergency bypass" access. When she calls, she gets through.

Furthermore, if my intention is to deeply focus on a project for hours at a time, I'll activate airplane mode. When enabled, it's like being in a black hole. I'll set my timer for an hour at a time, and when the alarm goes off, I'll take a break. I'll check for urgent voicemails, emails and text messages. I'll get up to move my body and use the bathroom if needed. But once I'm done, I'm right back into airplane mode for another hyper-focused hour.

Schedule a Block for That

So that nothing goes unanswered, I add recurring blocks to my schedule for outreach. These blocks remind me to check back into the real world every few hours.

As for my email usage, there are two recurring blocks on my calendar acting as reminders for me to check in. Twice a day, for fifteen minutes, I read and reply to emails.

You may think it's crazy to check email only twice a day. Maybe for you it is. If you're in the customer support business, for instance, this approach wouldn't work. In fact, you could get fired for checking your email so infrequently! Be sure you're taking into consideration your unique circumstances.

Once you identify your worst offender, you don't have to eliminate it entirely from your life if you don't want to. Try scheduling a few blocks in your calendar where you can focus on and enjoy whatever it is. In other words, be more *intentional* about these types of distractions!

If you enjoy binging on your favorite series on Netflix, schedule it. But make sure it's during the *appropriate* time of day. Not when you should be working, connecting with your significant other or investing time with your children. When it's time to binge, enter those blocks on your schedule and enjoy every minute of it.

Please don't feel guilty about enjoying your distractions. If we all focused on being effective 100 percent of the time, we'd burn out. We all need a healthy amount of variety and distraction in our lives. "Downtime" is necessary. What's important here is that we're not investing too much of our time in this dimension of distraction.

Be honest with yourself here. What distracts you the most? Once you identify your worst offender, come up with a plan to eliminate it so you can regain control of your attention throughout the day.

Once you've regained control of your attention and created a focus-rich environment, you'll begin experiencing significant progress on your highest priorities. Before you know it, the grades in every area of your life will improve exponentially.

It's now time to envision a compelling future for your life by defining clear, meaningful goals. We'll cover *how* to best approach this in the next chapter.

Key Points

- By treating your daily environment like a virtual classroom, you can safeguard your attention from an endless sea of distraction.
- Most of us are exposed to hundreds, if not thousands, of marketing messages every day. Furthermore, recent reports suggest that the average U.S. adult spends just under four hours per day on their mobile device.
- Your attention is the number one asset you have. It's up

to each and every one of us to protect our attention like it's gold, because it is.

- With a little effort, you can control many of the things that distract you in our daily environment.
- It's important to identify your worst offender, the distraction that interrupts your focus the most.
- By coming up with a plan to eliminate your biggest distraction, you can regain control of your attention throughout the day.
- We all need a healthy amount of variety and distraction in our lives, but what's important here is that you're not investing too much of your time in this dimension of distraction.

Chapter Assignment

1. Identify your worst offender (the distraction that interrupts your focus the most).
2. Research ways you can overcome it.
3. Put a plan in place to reduce or remove it from your daily routine (or be more intentional about it by scheduling it during the appropriate time).
4. With your worst offender defeated, pay attention to how much time, focus and energy you're reinvesting into your highest priorities.

8

MAJORS, MINORS & ELECTIVES
DEFINING CLEAR, MEANINGFUL GOALS

"You are never too old to set another goal or to dream a new dream."

— C.S. LEWIS

Think back to grade school for a moment. Wasn't the thought of progressing to the next grade exciting? Those "older kids" seemed so much bigger and more mature than we were. As long as we continued to advance toward the next grade, we'd become those "older kids" in no time.

In high school, maybe you were excited to finish formal education and enter the workforce. Or perhaps you were excited to move out of the house, continuing your education by attending college.

If you chose the collegiate path, you eventually selected a major area of study. This major area of study helped you advance in the direction of whatever career you were hoping to pursue.

The point is this: there was usually something right around the corner that *excited* us.

Having a compelling future to look forward to is something we should all strive for in the real world as well. Without a compelling future, we run the risk of experiencing what Viktor Frankl called the "existential vacuum."[1]

This is that feeling where you're questioning your purpose in life. You feel like you're going through the motions, drifting in an endless sea of distraction and settling for a life that lacks meaning.

This is dangerous territory, and we want to avoid it at all costs.

I experienced this existential vacuum for nearly ten years, between the ages of eighteen and twenty-eight. I was utterly lost. I'm not proud of the choices I made during this period of my life. These choices, as I shared in the introduction, led to what I now view as my multifaceted bankruptcy.

Defining What You Want

Defining what we want in life can instantly propel us out of this existential vacuum.

There is a psychological benefit as well. When you define what you want in life, you activate a certain function in your brain called the Reticular Activation System, or "RAS" for short. It helps you identify opportunities in your environment which move you closer to obtaining whatever it is you desire.

Amazingly, our five senses send *eleven million* bits of information to our brains *every second*. Our conscious mind can only process *fifty* of these eleven million bits each second.[2] Your RAS acts as a filter, helping you focus exclusively on the information relevant to your ability to survive or thrive.

I bet you've experienced your RAS in action. Remember the last time you wanted to buy something? Maybe it was a new piece of technology, a new pair of shoes, or a new car. Whatever it was, I'll bet you began noticing it everywhere you looked.

Once you defined what you wanted, your RAS had the necessary instruction to *seek it out of your environment* and bring it to your attention.

You can put your RAS to good use by envisioning a compelling future for your life. By doing so, not only will you ignite that inner sense of excitement that you get when you have something to look forward to, but you will also increase the chances of your desired future becoming your reality.

The Lay of the Land

When students attend college, they aren't asked to declare their major on the first day of school. In fact, most college students don't declare their major until their sophomore or junior year.

Why?

Because college students must get a better understanding of how college life works. They must uncover all the options available to them. They have to become familiar with the lay of the land before making a rather difficult decision: declaring their majors.

My hope is that you, too, have become more familiar with the layout of the land as it pertains to this approach. We've come a long way since the first chapter, which is why I feel it's important to take a moment to review everything we've covered thus far.

In Chapter 1, you learned how to discover the areas of your life that matter most.

In Chapter 2, you learned how to objectively assess these areas by assigning a letter grade to each one.

In Chapter 3, you learned how to identify your highest priorities.

In Chapter 4, you learned how to organize these priorities.

In Chapter 5, you learned how to live proactively instead of reactively by performing the weekly review.

In Chapter 6, you learned how to make the most of your time by performing the daily plan and adding structure to your day.

In Chapter 7, you learned how to eliminate your major distractions and create a more focus-rich environment that is conducive to your success.

If you're taking the time to complete the assignments at the end of each chapter, I'll bet you're beginning to experience significant progress in most (if not all) areas of your life.

This entire approach was designed intentionally to help you experience progress *first*. We all know it's hard to focus on the future when we're in "survival mode." When we're struggling to keep our heads above water and simply doing our best to make it to tomorrow, taking the time to define meaningful goals can seem rather irrelevant.

If this describes you, I encourage you to go back and review the previous chapters. Take as much time as you need to complete the assignments. They're in a very specific order for a very important reason: to help you move away from survival mode toward a place of stability as quickly as possible.

When you're ready, and you're experiencing real progress in the areas of your life that matter most, it's time to envision a compelling future by defining clear and meaningful goals.

When to Define Goals

As a general rule, when there are less than sixty days left in the calendar year, consider defining your goals for the following year. If there are more than sixty days left in the year, consider defining your goals within the current year.

For instance, if you're reading this book between November 1st and December 31st, it would make the most sense to define your goals for the following year. If you're reading this book between January 1st and October 31st, consider doing a "practice round" and define your goals for the current year.

Here's a little secret: the timing doesn't matter. What does matter is the practice of defining clear, meaningful goals as soon as possible. Practice breeds experience. The more experience you have, the better you'll become at defining clear and meaningful goals over time.

Less is Always More

In college, every student must eventually declare his or her major. A very small percentage of students declare a minor, and even fewer pursue a double major. These are the exceptions and not the rule. The vast majority of students don't have the interest, the mental bandwidth or the time capacity to pursue more than one discipline at a time.

Why, then, do so many of us define so many goals for ourselves every year in the real world?

Years ago, I assumed I could pursue many goals throughout the year. Back then, I was managing eleven areas of life, and I defined eleven goals for the coming year. How many did I actually accomplish? Only two, and I felt like these two goals were done in a half-measured sort of way.

In other words, I wasn't satisfied with my results.

You see, when everything is important, nothing is important. When everything must get done, nothing tends to get done.

We fail to recognize that everything comes down to our ability to *focus*. When we're focused on too many things at the same time, everything suffers.

Take a 100-watt lightbulb, for example. When used in our homes, it lights up a room rather nicely. A 100-watt laser, on the other hand, can cut through steel. Both use the same energy, but the results are dramatically different. The only difference here is how the energy is *focused*. The same rules apply to the goals you define for the year.

As you define your goals, I strongly encourage you to take a "less is more" approach. Keep things simple and start small so you can focus your energy and maximize your results.

Defining Your Goals

Take a moment to review the areas of your life. Do you see any areas where you could define a specific annual goal?

There are probably one, two or three areas where it would make sense to do so. For instance, you might see an opportunity to define a health, wealth and relationship goal. Once you've identified these areas, it's time to define clear, meaningful goals for the year.

Take a few moments to think through the goal within each area. What is your ideal outcome? Where would you like to be within this area of your life at the end of the year?

Picture your ideal outcome in your mind's eye and do your best to capture it in a sentence. Make it as specific as possible so you'll be crystal clear as to whether or not you've accomplished it.

If you need some extra guidance on defining your goals, perform a quick search on Google for "SMART goals."

Declaring Your Major and Minor(s)

This year, I defined three goals within three areas of my life: Marriage, Mission (work) and Wealth.

Once I defined these goals, I took a step back and reviewed them from a distance. I asked myself if accomplishing just *one* of these goals could change *everything* for me this year. The answer was "yes." I realized the goal I had defined in the Mission area of my life would not only support my Wealth goal, but it would also support my Marriage goal.

If I accomplished this one goal, it would act as the tide, lifting all my boats. I declared this my "major" goal for the year. The other two became my "minor" goals.

If you define more than one goal across multiple areas of your life, take a step back. Review each goal and decide which one, if accomplished, could change *everything* for you this year. Declare this as your "major" goal for the year and declare the others as your "minor" goals for the year.

Never Overlook Your Electives

I treat the other areas of my life, the ones where I didn't define annual goals, as "electives." These areas are still important to me, and I can't afford to overlook them, otherwise, I'll run the risk of imbalance if all I do is focus on the areas where I've defined goals for the year.

What are your electives? Never overlook them. You'll want to continually manage and improve these areas throughout the year.

Rest assured you won't lose sight of these areas if you're performing the weekly review. If you recall, I encouraged you to assess *all* the areas of your life at the beginning of this agenda.

Like college students declaring their majors, you should have a clear vision of your compelling future once you define meaningful goals for the year. Now it's time to take the first step toward making this future of yours a reality.

In the next chapter, we'll learn how to overcome procrastination by breaking these goals down into manageable projects and steps.

Key Points

- Without a compelling future, we run the risk of experiencing what Viktor Frankl called the "existential vacuum."
- Defining what we want in life can instantly propel us out of this existential vacuum.
- When you define what you want, you activate a certain function in your brain called the Reticular Activation System, or "RAS" for short. It helps you identify opportunities in your environment that move you closer toward obtaining whatever it is you desire.
- It's hard to focus on the future when we're in "survival mode." When we're struggling to keep our heads above water and simply doing our best to make it to tomorrow, taking the time to define meaningful goals can seem rather irrelevant.

- When it comes to defining goals, the timing doesn't necessarily matter. What does matter is the practice of defining clear, meaningful goals as soon as possible. Practice breeds experience. The more experience you have, the better you'll become at defining clear and meaningful goals over time.
- Everything comes down to our ability to *focus*. When we're focused on too many things at the same time, everything suffers.
- As you define your goals for the year, take a "less is more" approach. Keep things simple and start small so you can focus your energy and maximize your results.
- Once you declare your major and minor goals for the year, never overlook your electives. You'll want to continually manage and improve these other areas of your life throughout the year. Rest assured you won't lose sight of these areas if you're performing the weekly review.

∾

Chapter Assignment

1. Review all the areas of your life and identify one, two, or three areas where you could define goals for the year.
2. Define clear, meaningful goals within these areas.
3. Identify the one goal that could change everything. Declare this your "major" goal for the year and the others your "minor" goals for the year.
4. Never overlook your "electives." You'll want to continually manage and improve all your areas of life throughout the year. Consider assessing every area of

your life on a weekly basis during your weekly review.

9

LESSON PLANS
OVERCOMING PROCRASTINATION

"Planning is bringing the future into the present so that you can do something about it now."

— ALAN LAKEIN

D o you remember those enormous textbooks in school? They were incredibly intimidating.

Luckily, the teacher came prepared with *lesson plans*. The purpose of these lesson plans was to lay out the curriculum in a timely, space-based manner. This gave my fellow classmates and me a greater chance of staying on track with our studies.

Lesson plans dictated what we learned, when we learned and how we learned throughout the school year.

Lesson plans are just as important in the real world as they were in school, but many of us fail to create them in our own lives. When we don't take the time to create lesson plans to support our major and minor goals, the chances of our actually accomplishing these goals decrease significantly.

By creating lesson plans, we'll know *which* projects we need to focus on to support our goals as well as *when* we'll need to focus on them. Furthermore, we'll have a good handle on the key steps that require our attention as we begin chipping away at our projects.

Identifying these projects and steps ahead of time can also help us to overcome procrastination as we begin working toward our major and minor goals for the year.

Let's face it, staring at a big goal or major project can be paralyzing. If we focus on that next small step in front of us, we'll have a greater chance of immediately taking action and maintaining that forward momentum.

As Lao Tzu, the ancient Chinese philosopher writes in the *Tao te Ching*, "The journey of a thousand miles begins with a single step."[1]

Breaking Goals Down into Manageable Projects

In the last chapter, we identified your major and minor goals for the year. These goals can appear quite intimidating, and they can leave us feeling overwhelmed, but it doesn't have to be this way. Let's break these goals down into manageable projects throughout the year.

Begin with your major goal. What are some projects you'll have to focus on over the course of the year to accomplish it? Think big picture here. We're looking for the "rocks," as Stephen Covey so elegantly demonstrated when he graced us on stage.[2] These are the projects that matter the most in your life; the ones that support your major and minor goals.

For example, my family is currently in the process of moving. It's a major goal for us this year. Our ideal outcome is to be settled into our new home, but a lot has to happen between now and then.

If we were to identify the projects that support this goal, we might come up with three:

Project #1: Sell

Project #2: Search

Project #3: Settle In

First, we'll have to go through the motion of selling our existing home. Second, we'll have to search for a new home while we rent in an unfamiliar city and get acquainted with the area. Finally, after purchasing a new house, we'll have to get settled in and make ourselves at home.

This is a simplified example, but you get the idea. Moving is a major undertaking, but "chunking" it down into manageable projects helps make it seem a little less intimidating. Decreasing the intimidation factor decreases the chances of being held back by procrastination.

Once you've taken the time to break your major goal down into projects, it's time to decide *when* you'll want to focus on each project. An ideal strategy is when you can compartmentalize each of your projects into the four quarters of the year.

However, if your major goal is like the moving example above, certain factors may be outside of your control.

In a perfect world, we'd sell our home in the first quarter of the year. Then, in the second quarter, we'd search for and close on a new property. Finally, in the third quarter, we'd settle into our new home and make it our own.

Certain goals, like moving, as well as the projects that support them, can't be compartmentalized into quarters. Sometimes too many factors are outside of your control. Be aware of this and remain flexible as you consider the timing on these types of goals and projects.

A good example of a major goal where the projects *can* be compartmentalized into quarters is losing weight. If you wanted to lose fifty pounds this year, you could set a weight target for each quarter and treat these weight targets as projects. Assuming you accomplish your projects each quarter, you'll be on track to accomplish your major goal for the year.

After you identify the projects that support your major goal, see if they align well with the four quarters of the year. If so, do your best to compartmentalize these projects over the next few quarters. Which projects will you focus on during each quarter?

If the projects you identify don't align well with the four quarters of the year, simply arrange them in sequential order. Make a rough estimate on when you'll focus on these projects over the next few months or quarters.

When you take the time to brainstorm the projects that will support your major goal, it often leads to that *Aha!* feeling you get when you put plans on paper. In *Think & Grow Rich*, Napoleon Hill writes, "The most intelligent man living cannot succeed in accumulating money – nor in any other undertaking – without plans which are practical and workable."[3]

Your projects are the beginning stages of your own practical and workable plans. These are the plans that will support you throughout the entire year.

Invest some time brainstorming which projects will support your major goal.

1,000 True Fans

In the last chapter, I shared a bit about my major goal for this year. It has to do with the Mission (work) area of my life. I decided that if I could accomplish this major goal, it would support my minor goals for the year as well.

My major goal for this year is this:

Launch a Business Model that Leverages My Unique Abilities & Contributes to 1,000 True Fans in a Meaningful Way.

This major goal is well-defined and specific. I'll know, with absolute certainty, whether I accomplish this goal by year's end.

When I defined this major goal, I was intimidated. Launching a new business requires a lot of effort. Saying goodbye to a fifteen-year career in another industry is uncomfortable. Entering into a new market is scary. Putting myself out there on the internet is conflicting because I value my privacy. Finding one thousand true fans when the only true fan I have is my own mother seems silly and unrealistic.

I could have easily self-talked my way out of this one. Instead, I used that same energy to brainstorm a list of projects that would support my major goal.

My initial list of projects looked something like this:

- Develop an online course
- Publish a handful of success guides on YouTube
- Write a book
- Design and execute marketing campaigns for book and course
- Acquire 1,000 "true fans"
- Create and publish a planner
- Host a live event/mastermind

- Launch a website
- Build a Facebook page
- Build a YouTube channel

At the beginning of the year, it was difficult to predict which projects would support my major goal. I realize these projects are subject to change over time, but I needed a practical and workable place to *start*.

I took a few more minutes to decide which projects I'd focus on throughout the year by compartmentalizing them by quarter. As I went through this motion, the language I used to describe my initial list of projects changed a bit and became more personal. I also combined some of the projects together in an effort to simplify.

Quarter 1:

- Write my book

Quarter 2:

- Launch my website, Facebook and YouTube presence
- Publish my first success guide on YouTube
- Publish my book
- Develop and launch my online course
- Design & execute marketing campaigns for my book and course

Quarter 3:

- Manage marketing campaigns for my book and course
- Publish another success guide on YouTube
- Design & execute campaign to acquire my 1,000 "true fans"

Quarter 4:

- Manage marketing campaigns for my book and course
- Publish another success guide on YouTube
- Manage campaign to acquire my 1,000 "true fans"

Compartmentalizing my projects by quarter forced me to arrange my projects in sequential order. Doing so helped me gain a better understanding of which ones demanded my time and attention first.

I realized that without a book, I don't have a business model. And that's my "north star" for the year: to launch a new business model. Thanks to this realization, I'm focusing all my efforts on writing a book in the first quarter.

I've since dropped two of the projects I initially came up with. Hosting a live event or mastermind isn't possible as we're currently living in the middle of the coronavirus pandemic. Creating and publishing a planner is a neat idea but doesn't directly support my annual goal. It's a "nice to have," but not necessary, at least not this year. I simply placed these two projects in the parking lot section within the Mission area of my life for future reference.

Will this year go exactly as planned, the same way I had anticipated at the onset of the year?

Definitely not.

In fact, I've already had to change gears a few times. Outside circumstances have interfered on numerous occasions, and timelines have been moved around. I've had to course-correct more often than I could have imagined over the past ninety days (more on *how* to do this in the next chapter).

For now, it's important to brainstorm the projects that will support your major goal. If you don't take the time to do this now, you run the risk of feeling intimidated later. When we're intimidated, procrastination becomes a force that is hard to reckon with.

Once you've identified the projects that support your major goal, repeat the same process for your minor goals (if applicable).

Breaking Projects Down into Manageable Steps

After identifying relevant projects for the coming month or quarter, it's time to break these projects down into manageable steps.

Start by looking at the first project on your list. What are all the steps necessary to accomplish it? Make a list of these steps and be sure you've arranged them in the appropriate order. Do your best to determine how much time each step will require. Finally, assign a due date to each step.

These steps simply become *priorities* in the weeks they're due.

Following along from my previous example, I have one project in the first quarter of the year. Write my book. Breaking this project into steps might look something like this:

1. Identify resources/training
2. Devour resources/training
3. Identify next steps

Since writing a book is uncharted territory for me, these are the only steps I could identify at the beginning of the year.

By chance, they're already in order. Now I must determine how much time each step will take:

1. Identify resources/training - 5 hours
2. Devour resources/training - TBD
3. Identify next steps – TBD

I don't know how long the second and thirds step will actually take just yet, so I'll add a "TBD" next to those steps for now.

Finally, I'll assign due dates for each step:

1. Identify resources/training - 5 hours (Jan 10)
2. Devour resources/training - TBD (Jan 31)
3. Identify next steps - TBD (Jan 31)

In this example, I'll identify the right resources and training for writing a book by the 10th of January. This gives me a week and a half to do my due diligence around this topic. Then, I'll have about three weeks to devour whatever resources or training I find most relevant. Assuming I accomplish my learning by the 31st of January, I'll wait until then to identify my next steps. With two months left in the first quarter of the year, I'll have sixty days to plan, write and edit my book.

Since the beginning of the year, a lot has changed with this initial plan, but I'm still on track. It's late-March as I edit this paragraph and put the finishing touches on my manuscript.

Do you see how powerful an exercise like this can be?

If we don't take the time to break our projects down into manageable steps, we procrastinate. And when we procrastinate, we run the risk of blowing our deadlines. When deadlines get extended, projects won't get accomplished on time. And when projects aren't accomplished on time, it's impossible to achieve our goals for the year.

It's another example of the compound effect, but unlike the one referred to in Chapter 6, this one's moving in the opposite direction. Momentum is a powerful force regardless of its polarity.

"But My Situation is Different"

If you don't think this is possible due to your unique situation or existing schedule, please reconsider.

This is one of those "if I can do it, so can you" scenarios.

At the beginning of the year, I had an incredibly positive outlook on life and business. I spent the majority of last year getting my other business as close to "autopilot" as possible in preparation for this year. In January, my schedule was clear, and the first quarter was earmarked for writing my book.

Best laid plans, right?

Fast-forward a few short months, and the entire world is going through a pandemic. Like so many others have recently experienced, the safety net of my income has completely vanished. School has been canceled indefinitely, and my wife has taken on the role of full-time teacher. All extracurricular activities have been canceled as the entire world is under quarantine.

To complicate matters even further, my wife and I have made the sudden decision to move to a different state. A few short weeks ago, this move was ten or more years out. Thanks to some unforeseen circumstances, it's now within a ninety-day window.

To be clear, I'm not complaining. Luckily, we all have our health, and for that I'm truly grateful.

I share these details with you to drive home this point:

I've had to adjust my plans over, and over and over.

When I first started writing my book, I was in a private office environment. When writing from there was no longer an option, I'd write from my favorite local coffee shop. Since they've been forced to close their doors, I'm now writing from an empty spare bedroom at my in-laws' house. I set up a plastic folding table on the bare floor and pulled up a chair.

No joke.

I've also had to adjust my schedule on an *hourly* basis. Some days, I've written at 4 a.m. when everyone else was still sleeping. Other days, I've written at 1 p.m. when two of my three children were napping and my oldest son was on a screen. Have I felt guilty about putting him on a screen so I could get back to my writing? You better believe it. I've also written on numerous evenings around 9 p.m. when our home was finally quiet despite having zero energy after another long day of quarantine.

The point is this: no matter what your current situation is or what your schedule looks like, you too can break your important projects down into manageable steps. And you can focus on and accomplish these steps, one by one, under *any* conditions (including a pandemic).

Benchmark the Status of Your Projects During the Weekly Review

I hope by now you're in the habit of performing your weekly review. If so, you can use this time to benchmark the status of your projects and decide which steps you'll focus on for the coming week.

When one of the steps that supports a project has a due date within the next seven days, it simply becomes a *priority* you'll focus on that week.

This is an effective way to ensure the projects that support your major and minor goals are consistently on track.

Taking the time to create your own lesson plans for the year isn't easy, but it's well worth the effort. I hope you'll identify the projects that support your major and minor goals, as well as identify the steps that support your upcoming projects.

In the next chapter, you'll learn a simple way to course-correct throughout the year when life inevitably gets off-track.

Key Points

- When you don't take the time to create lesson plans to support our major and minor goals, the chances of accomplishing these goals decreases significantly.
- Identifying the projects and steps that support your major and minor goals helps you to overcome procrastination as you begin working toward them.
- If you focus solely on that next small step in front of you, you'll have a greater chance of immediately taking action and maintaining forward momentum.
- Momentum is a powerful force regardless of its polarity.
- No matter what your current situation is or what your schedule looks like, you can break your important projects down into manageable steps. And you can

focus on and accomplish these steps, one by one, under any conditions (including a pandemic).

- You can use the time during your weekly review to check-in on the status of your projects and decide which steps you'll focus on for the coming week. This is an effective way to ensure the projects that support your major and minor goals are consistently on track.

Chapter Assignment

1. Break your major and minor goals down into manageable projects.
2. Decide when you'll focus on each project and compartmentalize them by quarter (if applicable).
3. Break your upcoming projects down into manageable steps. Make sure the steps for each project are arranged in the appropriate order. Decide how much time you'll need to accomplish each step and assign a due date for each one.
4. Don't forget to benchmark the status of your projects during your weekly review and decide which steps you'll focus on for the coming week.

10

RETREATS

COURSE-CORRECTING THROUGHOUT THE YEAR

"You've got to think about big things while you're doing small things, so that all the small things go in the right direction."

— ALVIN TOFFLER

As you close in on the final chapters of this book, take a moment to appreciate all the ground you've covered over the last few chapters.

In Chapter 7, you learned how to eliminate your major distractions and create a focus-rich environment conducive to your success.

In Chapter 8, you learned how to define clear, meaningful goals for the year that support your compelling future.

In the previous chapter, you learned how to overcome procrastination by breaking these goals down into manageable projects and steps.

You're on a roll, but eventually you may need a break from your daily routine. Do you remember taking these breaks in school? You probably referred to them as field trips or *retreats*.

As students, these retreats were like a welcomed breath of fresh air. Some retreats added a new element of learning relating back to a specific subject area. Others provided us with a fresh perspective on life while allowing us to blow off a little steam.

Retreats serve an important purpose for us in the real world, too. The problem, of course, is that many of us don't invest the time to take them as often as we should. When we fail to break from our daily routine for some fresh perspective, we risk losing sight of our progress as it relates to the compelling future we've envisioned for our lives.

By taking retreats, we give ourselves a chance to course-correct our goals and projects as life inevitably gets off-track throughout the year.

Think about this for a moment. In the previous two chapters, you learned how to define meaningful goals and break them down into manageable projects and steps.

I'm willing to bet you've done an exercise like this in the past. You're all excited about the goals you've defined, but then you enter back into your daily routine and those goals get left behind.

Life got in the way again.

Does this resonate with you?

Here's what we have to accept: our lives will inevitably get off-track. If we're not careful, our goals and projects get pushed to the side as we return to our daily routine. Life gets pretty chaotic at times, and it doesn't take much to lose sight of the big picture when we're constantly being pulled back into the weeds.

Performing Your Own Autopilot

In *How to Develop Your Personal Mission Statement*, Stephen Covey writes, "Think about taking a trip on an airplane. Before taking off, the pilot has a very clear destination in mind, which hopefully coincides with yours, and a flight plan to get there. The plane takes off at the appointed hour toward that predetermined destination. But in fact, the plane is off course at least 90 percent of the time. Weather conditions, turbulence and other factors cause it to get off track. However, feedback is given to the pilot constantly, who then makes course corrections and keeps coming back to the exact flight plan, bringing the plane back on course. And often, the plane arrives at the destination on time. It's amazing. Think of it. Leaving on time, arriving on time, but off course 90 percent of the time."[1]

Pilots also have the luxury of what's called *autopilot*. This function brings the airplane back on course, so it arrives on schedule at its destination. When activated, the pilots can relax, converse casually and even enjoy a meal together.

Life is like the flight of an airplane; it's off-course 90 percent of the time. Unfortunately, life doesn't come equipped with the autopilot function. We have to perform this function *manually*. Aside from parenting, I'd argue it's one of the most important jobs we have as human beings.

To do this effectively throughout the year, we'll have to go above and beyond performing the weekly review covered in Chapter 5. While the weekly review works well for short-term planning, it's now time for us to solve for our long-term planning needs.

The Quarterly Retreat

The quarterly retreat will help you manage and benchmark your projects more effectively. When your projects are on track, your major and minor goals for the year will be, too.

We'll take the same approach we took when adopting the weekly review in Chapter 5. Find a time in your schedule, either at the end of this quarter or at the beginning of the next quarter, where you can invest about ninety minutes to review the coming quarter.

In my experience, simply "extending" the time you're already investing in the weekly review works just fine. Since I perform my weekly review every Sunday, this is when I go on my quarterly retreat, but any day will do. As you'll soon notice, the agenda for the quarterly retreat simply builds upon the agenda from the weekly review.

Next, you'll want to block out the time in your planner or calendar. This will remind you that you've made a commitment to yourself to go on the quarterly retreat. If you use a digital calendar, set this block of time to repeat forever (just like you did with the weekly review).

Sample Agenda

Here's a sample agenda for your consideration:

What: The Quarterly Retreat

When: End or Beginning of Each Quarter

Where: Out in Nature / A Focus-Rich Environment

1. Assess the Areas of Your Life (10 minutes)
2. Review Calendar for the Coming Quarter (10 minutes)

3. Review Annual Goals & Projects (10 minutes)
4. Identify New Projects & Define Steps (30 minutes)
5. Review the Parking Lot for Each Life Area (5 minutes)
6. Review Calendar for the Coming Week (5 minutes)
7. Benchmark Projects & Identify Steps (10 minutes)
8. Identify Priorities & Assign Due Dates (10 minutes)

In this example, it'll take ninety minutes to go on the quarterly retreat.

For clarification purposes, let's review each item on this sample agenda.

Assess the Areas of Your Life

This helps you get a quick pulse on how well you're doing in every area of your life. Assign a letter grade to each area and calculate the updated GPA. If you discover a certain area to be significantly off-track, consider which actions you can take in the coming quarter to improve your grade. Make a note of these actions and recognize them as either projects or priorities you'll want to focus on over the next ninety days.

Review Calendar for the Coming Quarter

This helps you get a head-start on your quarter. Briefly review your calendar from a high level. Look for anything over the next ninety days you may need to plan for like holidays, birthdays and events. When you do find something you need to plan for, create an action, assign a due date and add it to your list of priorities in whichever area of life it applies.

Review Annual Goal(s) and Projects

Review each goal, one at a time. Is your goal, as well as the projects that support your goal, still relevant? Is everything still on track? If not, what adjustments should you make? Repeat this process for each goal. You're using this as an opportunity to course-correct. Take the necessary time to ensure your goals and projects are still in alignment.

Identify New Projects and Define Steps

You'll want to decide which projects to focus on over the next ninety days. Once you've made a decision, take the necessary time to break each project down into manageable steps. Arrange the steps in the appropriate order. Now, consider how much time each step will take. Finally, assign due dates for each step. This will help you get a jump start on your projects, and you'll enter the first week of the quarter already knowing exactly which steps to focus on. Feel free to reference Chapter 9 for more detailed instructions.

Review the Parking Lot for Each Life Area

Review the parking lot section within every area of your life (see Chapter 4, page 33). Decide if there are any new projects or priorities you want to focus on in the upcoming quarter. When you identify a new project, repeat the instructions from the previous step in the agenda. When you identify a new priority, assign a due date to it and remove it from the parking lot section.

The last three steps on the agenda should look familiar to you. They're the same steps from the weekly review. Feel free to reference Chapter 5 for further instruction.

Review Calendar for the Coming Week

Benchmark Projects & Identify Steps

Identify Priorities & Assign Due Dates

By taking the time to go on the quarterly retreat, you'll have a much greater chance at accomplishing your major and minor goals for the year.

If you're interested in using the same quarterly retreat agenda I use, you can download a customizable template at Intentional-Book.com.

The Annual Retreat

The annual retreat will help you step back, take inventory, and count your blessings over the previous year. It will also help you move forward into the new year with clarity around your intentions.

We'll take the same approach we took when adopting the weekly review and quarterly retreat. Find a time in your schedule, either at the end of this year or at the beginning of next year. You'll want to invest up to three hours to go on the annual retreat.

Again, simply "extending" the time you're already investing in the quarterly retreat works just fine. Since I go on my quarterly retreat on Sunday, this is when I go on my annual retreat as well. Remember, any day will do. The agenda for the annual retreat simply builds on the agenda from the quarterly retreat.

Next, you'll want to block out the time in your planner or calendar. This will remind you that you've made a commitment to yourself to go on the annual retreat. If you use a digital calendar, set this block of time to repeat forever (just like you did with the weekly review and the quarterly retreat).

Sample Agenda

Here's a sample agenda for your consideration:

What: The Annual Retreat

When: End or Beginning of Each Year

Where: Out in Nature / A Focus-Rich Environment

1. Assess the Areas of Your Life (10 minutes)
2. Identify Top 3 Blessings, Lessons and Breakthroughs from the Previous Year (20 minutes)
3. Review Last Year's Goals (10 minutes)
4. Define Annual Goal(s) for the Coming Year (20 minutes)
5. Break Annual Goals Down into Projects (20 minutes)
6. Identify New Projects & Define Steps (30 minutes)
7. Review Calendar for the Coming Quarter (10 minutes)
8. Review the Parking Lot for Each Life Area (5 minutes)
9. Review Calendar for the Coming Week (5 minutes)
10. Benchmark Projects & Identify Steps (10 minutes)
11. Identify Priorities & Assign Due Dates (10 minutes)

In this example, it will take three hours to go on the annual retreat.

For clarification purposes, let's review each item on this sample agenda.

Assess the Areas of Your Life

This helps you get a quick pulse on how well you're doing in every area of your life. Assign a letter grade to each area and calculate the updated GPA. You're locking in your final grades for the year. If you discover a certain area to be significantly off-track, consider which actions you can take in the coming year to improve your grade. Make a note of these actions and recognize them as either goals, projects or priorities you'll want to focus on over the next year.

Identify Top 3 Blessings, Lessons and Breakthroughs from the Previous Year

This helps you pause, reflect and take some time for introspection. As you think about the previous year, try to come up with the top three blessings you've experienced throughout the year. What are you grateful for? Come up with your top three lessons. What are the biggest lessons you've learned throughout the year? Finally, come up with your top three breakthroughs. Did you experience any breakthroughs? Use this as an opportunity to take as much inventory as you need from the previous year.

Review Last Year's Goals

This gives you the ability to see how well you did with your major and minor goals. How did you do? Calculate the completion ratio. For example, if you had three goals for the year and you completed two of the three, you would have a completion rate of 66 percent. Calculating the ratio often helps us recognize when we've taken on too many goals. It might serve as a good reminder to take a "less is more" approach when defining new major and minor goals for the coming year.

Define Annual Goal(s) for the Coming Year

It's time to define new and meaningful goals for the coming year. Start by reviewing all the areas of your life. Do certain areas make more sense in which to define goals than others? Decide which areas make the most sense. Define specific goals for these areas. Finally, identify the one goal that could change everything; this is the tide that lifts all boats. This becomes your major goal for the year. The other goals, if applicable, become your minor goals. Feel free to reference Chapter 8 for more detailed instruction.

Break Annual Goals Down into Projects

Use this as an opportunity to break your annual goals down into manageable projects. Begin with the major goal you defined for the year. What are some projects you'll have to focus on throughout the year to accomplish it? Decide when you'll want to focus on each project. Repeat the same process for your minor goals. Feel free to reference Chapter 9 for more detailed instructions.

The balance of the agenda should look familiar to you; they're the same steps from the quarterly retreat. Feel free to reference the sample agenda in the previous section of this chapter for further instruction.

Identify New Projects & Define Steps

Review Calendar for the Coming Quarter

Review the Parking Lot for Each Life Area

Review Calendar for the Coming Week

Benchmark Projects & Identify Steps

Identify Priorities & Assign Due Dates

Taking the time to go on the annual retreat will give you an opportunity to learn from your experiences in the previous year. It will also help you gain more clarity around your intentions for the year ahead.

Feel free to download the same annual retreat agenda I use and customize it to your liking at IntentionalBook.com.

While retreats gave us that much-needed perspective in school, they can provide us with the same benefit in the real world, too.

Now that you have everything you need to effectively course-correct throughout the year, we'll learn how you can exponentially accelerate your success in the next chapter.

Key Points

- By taking retreats, we give ourselves a chance to course-correct our goals and projects as life inevitably gets off-track throughout the year.
- Life is like the flight of an airplane; it's off-course 90 percent of the time.
- Life doesn't come equipped with the autopilot function. We have to perform this function manually. It's one of the most important jobs we have as human beings.
- By taking the time to go on the quarterly retreat, you'll have a much greater chance of accomplishing your major and minor goals for the year.
- Taking the time to go on the annual retreat will give you an opportunity to learn from your experiences in the previous year and help you gain more clarity around your intentions for the year ahead.

Chapter Assignment

1. Create your own quarterly and annual retreat agendas. You can download my customizable template at IntentionalBook.com.
2. Decide which days and times you'll commit to going on both retreats.

3. Block out these days and times in your planner or calendar (if you use a digital calendar, schedule a recurring block that repeats forever).

4. Go on the quarterly retreat once at the end of this quarter or beginning of next quarter and pay close attention to the results you experience.

5. Go on the annual retreat once at the end of this year or beginning of next year and pay close attention to the results you experience.

11
___

OFFICE HOURS
ACCELERATING YOUR SUCCESS

"Live as if you were to die tomorrow. Learn as if you were to live forever."

— MAHATMA GANDHI

During select times throughout the week, teachers make themselves available to help their students when they need extra guidance.

I remember visiting with my teachers often since I struggled so much in school. Like little local businesses, my teachers would hang their own "office hours" sign right outside their doors.

As students, help was readily available to us, but we had to have the *willingness* to ask for it. We also had to know where to *seek out* the right help.

This is more important now, in the real world, than it was in school. Back then, if we weren't willing to ask for help, and if we didn't know where to seek it out, it might've resulted in a bad grade. In the real world, the stakes are much higher, as that unwillingness could result in poor health, desperate financial circumstances or irreversible relationship troubles.

Thanks to the Information Age, we now have more access than ever to teachers who are willing to help. These teachers take on many disguises, including family members, friends, colleagues, therapists, authors, online trainers and seminar leaders.

Isn't it amazing to think that previous generations, when seeking access to knowledge, were limited to the shelves at their local libraries? These days we have access to the world's wisdom right in the palm of our hands, and it's expanding exponentially every day.

In fact, the online learning market is expected to reach a valuation of $325 *billion dollars* by the year 2025.[1]

While being granted unlimited access to the world's knowledge can be a good thing, it can also seem a little overwhelming at times.

The Congruency Factor

What if you could find the *right* teachers to help you significantly improve your grades in the areas of your life that matter most? Teachers who have already accomplished similar goals, empathize with the struggles you're facing and share your personal values and beliefs?

The key word here is *congruency*.

We need to seek out congruent teachers who can help us get from where we are to where we're hoping to be. The congruency factor is important, otherwise, we may not value or trust what these teachers are trying to teach us.

Have you ever learned from a teacher and then never applied the information he or she taught? Perhaps the congruency factor was missing.

My Money Makeover

It was clear I needed a lot of help in the financial area of my life. Shortly after my bankruptcy, I stumbled upon Dave Ramsey. After my initial research I felt congruent with Dave's values, beliefs and his overall approach.

I couldn't afford to attend one of his upcoming seminars, nor could I afford any of his online courses. Instead, I ended up purchasing his book, *The Total Money Makeover.*[2] In it, Dave delivered what the subtitle promised: A proven plan for financial fitness.

Because of the congruency factor, I not only invested the time to read his book, I also carefully applied each step of his plan in my own life.

His teachings continue to guide my financial decisions to this day.

Seeking Out Congruent Teachers

Right now, there are thousands of teachers ready, willing and able to help you in every single area of your life. All you have to do is have the willingness to ask for help and the ability to seek them out.

Start by reviewing the areas of your life. Which areas do you need the most help with? Which areas are you hoping to improve the most over the next few weeks or months?

Make a list of three to seven teachers for each area of life you're looking to improve. You probably know some teachers already, but if you come up short, do a quick Google search to see who else teaches in that space. Believe me, there are a lot of teachers out there who you haven't heard of just yet.

Once you've compiled your initial list of teachers, find out what types of resources they offer.

I like to search Amazon for bestselling books that apply to whichever area of life I'm looking to improve. I then visit the websites of these authors to see what other resources they offer. I'll usually find all sorts of good information, including webinars, audio programs, online courses and live events.

If you're new to doing this type of research, you might feel a little overwhelmed by the vast amount of information you discover. This is a normal response; it *is* overwhelming. For now, all you're looking to do is compile a list of all the potential resources you could tap into.

Once you've identified the teachers and the available resources they offer, get to know them a little better. Invest more time on their websites and consume some of their information. Many of these teachers have downloadable guides, YouTube channels and podcasts. The goal is to make sure *congruency* exists between the two of you.

This may seem like a big step, but it's worth it. I speak from experience here as I've invested a lot of time and money in self-education over the years. One of the two major reasons I've failed to follow through and apply what I've learned can be attributed to a lack of congruency with the teacher.

The other reason has to do with *relevancy*.

The Relevancy Factor

Now that you've compiled your initial list of teachers and the resources they offer, decide which resources are *relevant*. In other words, don't go out and buy a bunch of resources if you aren't going to consume and apply the information right away.

To help you determine which resources are relevant, think about the projects you're focused on. Will any of the resources you identified help you move these projects forward faster?

What about the areas of your life where you're struggling the most? When you're failing in one area it can feel like an urgent need. Can any of these resources help you improve your grade in an accelerated manner?

When a resource is sufficiently relevant, you'll have a greater chance of learning and applying it immediately.

I speak from experience here. I've invested tens of thousands of dollars in self-education over the years, and I've wasted a lot of money on limited-time "deals" even though the education wasn't relevant at the time. It then sits and collects dust.

Books, audio programs and online trainings can stack up awfully fast when you're not paying attention to the relevancy factor. I don't know about you, but this creates unnecessary stress in my life. I wind up feeling obligated (since I already paid for them) to pay attention to these resources at times in my life when they aren't even applicable.

Does this sound familiar?

Learning a New Love Language

A few years into my marriage, I felt like I was saying and doing all the right things, but for some unknown reason I didn't feel like my wife appreciated my efforts.

I became curious as to why I felt this way. When my curiosity turned into an urgent need, I went in search of a solution. I eventually discovered Gary Chapman's book, *The 5 Love Languages: The Secret to Love that Lasts.*[3]

Once again, before I invested the time to read his book, I did a little due diligence on Gary's website. After feeling like the congruency factor checked out, I purchased his book. I read it from cover to cover and *loved* it. I applied his teachings immediately, as the solution was highly relevant to the problem I faced in my own life.

What I learned fascinated me: we all have our own "languages of love," and for the past few years, I had failed to "speak" my wife's primary love language.

Over the next few weeks, I adjusted my "language" and began to see immediate results. My wife was so pleased that she, too, took an interest. She read the book, discovered my primary language and reciprocated beautifully.

As a result, the health of our marriage has improved dramatically.

Categorize Your Learning

Let's say you've identified a congruent teacher, and you've identified the most relevant resource that teacher offers. Now you'll need to decide if learning and applying this new resource is a project or a priority.

If you recall from Chapter 4, a project is an action that requires more than one step and more than two weeks of your focus to complete. A priority is more of a to-do that takes anywhere from a few minutes to a few hours.

Reading a book and implementing a few of the book's teachings might be viewed as a priority. You can do this in a week or two, especially if you're a fast reader and it's a short book. On the other hand, consuming an entire online course, along with all the written exercises, might be more of a project. This may take more than two weeks and span over the course of many months.

Last year, I purchased *Ultimate Relationship Program*[4] from Tony Robbins in the hope it would strengthen my marriage even further. With ten CDs and DVDs averaging about ninety minutes each, I knew this would take me over two weeks to learn and apply, so I treated this as a project.

I spaced my learning and application of this resource over a period of ninety days. Had I treated this as a priority, I might have started the program and experienced sheer overwhelm. If this were the case, I would have placed it back on the shelf for a later date. In my life, this later date usually translates to *never*.

Instead, I recognized it as a project and planned accordingly.

What you're trying to do here is *categorize* the resources you've identified. This will help you plan effectively so you have a greater chance of learning and, most importantly, applying your upcoming education.

While our teachers held specific office hours in school, most teachers in the real world are open twenty-four-seven. The trick is finding *congruent* teachers who offer *relevant* resources. When these two factors come together, we can succeed faster than ever before and improve the grades in every area of our lives.

In the final chapter, we'll discuss how to accelerate your learning and growth on an entirely new level.

Key Points

- You must have a willingness to ask for help and the ability to seek it out.
- Thanks to the Information Age, you now have more access than ever to teachers who are willing to help.
- You need to seek out congruent teachers who can help you get from where you are to where you're hoping to be. The congruency factor is important; otherwise, you may not value or trust what it is these teachers are trying to teach you.
- When a resource you've identified is sufficiently relevant, you'll have a greater chance of learning and applying it immediately.
- Categorizing the resources you've identified as either projects or priorities enables you to plan your upcoming education more effectively.

$\sim$

Chapter Assignment

1. Review the areas of your life and decide which areas you'd like to improve most over the next few weeks or months.
2. Compile a list of three to seven teachers who can help you improve your grades in these areas.
3. Investigate each teacher to determine if the congruency factor exists.

4. Where there is congruency, compile a list of resources offered by each teacher.
5. Determine which resources are relevant.
6. Where the relevancy factor exists, categorize these resources as either projects or priorities.
7. Plan effectively so you can learn and apply your upcoming education.

12

EXTRACURRICULAR ACTIVITIES
TAKING YOUR LEARNING AND GROWTH TO A NEW LEVEL

"If you want to go quickly, go alone. If you want to go far, go together."

— AFRICAN PROVERB

I n school, I was involuntarily immersed in a community of like-minded peers. We were all looking to achieve common objectives: get good grades and pass classes.

At a more advanced level, some students got involved in extracurricular activities like sports, band and other clubs. If you were one of those students, you remember what it felt like to surround yourself with like-minded people striving toward the same goal.

Surrounding ourselves with like-minded people is just as important in the real world as it was in school. By doing so, we not only take our learning and growth to an entirely new level, but we also advance toward our goals much faster than we can on our own.

I'll bet you already do this to some extent.

If you have a job, you're surrounded by coworkers on a daily basis. You have a common purpose to do business together, serve customers and grow the company.

If you're a full-time parent, I'll bet you surround yourself with other full-time parents. You have a common purpose of sharing your struggles and best practices relating to what I believe is the hardest (and most important) job on the planet.

If you're into wellness, you're probably surrounded by others who value their health, too. You have a common purpose of getting together to learn more about nutrition and help one another maintain active lifestyles.

As you learned in the previous chapter, seeking out the right teachers can help you succeed faster. But what else can you do to take your learning and growth to an entirely new level?

It's time to think more intentionally about the communities you can connect with on your journey. There are folks out there who share your *exact same* struggles and ambitions. By connecting with the people within these communities, you can accelerate your learning and growth faster than you could ever do on your own.

Memberships, Associations & Clubs

Are there any memberships, associations, or clubs you could join in your local area?

For instance, you might have access to a local chamber of commerce. By becoming a member, you can connect with other like-minded businesspeople. These businesspeople are also looking to expand their networks and grow their businesses too.

There are also clubs which focus on skillset development. If you wanted to develop your public speaking skills, for example, Toastmasters exists in most major cities. You can connect with other like-minded people who are hoping to overcome their fear and improve their public speaking skills.

Think about your major and minor goals. Also take into consideration the areas of your life that you're looking to improve this year. Would joining a membership, association or a club benefit you in any way?

Take some time to research the options available to you in your local area.

Classes

Another great option for meeting like-minded people is by participating in a class.

Let's say you're hoping to improve your cooking abilities. I'll bet there are some local classes you could register for. By doing so, you'll meet other people just like you who are looking to enhance their skills in the kitchen.

If you're looking to lose some weight, I'll bet there are endless classes you could join at your local gym or community center. There you'll meet other people just like you who are looking to get in shape and improve their health.

Think about the areas of your life you're looking to improve. Would participating in a class that relates to a specific area benefit you in any way?

If so, take some time to research which classes are available to you in your local area.

Accountability Partners

Do you struggle to follow through on your commitments?

I know I do.

Years ago, I realized I was making a lot of commitments but following through on very little. I decided to reach out to a few friends to see if they had any interest in connecting regularly for the purpose of holding one another accountable. These friends agreed. We've been meeting consistently every two weeks for over three years now. We connect on the same day, at the same time and follow the same agenda. Over the years, the time we've invested together has helped us become more accountable than we could have been our own.

Think of someone you know who shares similar goals or is hoping to improve similar areas in life. Would connecting on a regular basis for the purpose of holding one another accountable be of benefit to you (and to him/her)?

Book Clubs

For the past few years, my wife has gotten together with a group of girlfriends every month. They call it "book club," but from my vantage point it looks more like *wine club*. I've always admired their ability to make time for one another, connect on a deeper level and discuss a topic with which they have a shared interest: fiction.

I searched for a similar book club in my local area. Instead of reading fiction, however, I was more interested in reading non-fiction. When my search came up short, I decided to start my own. I sent an email to nine of my closest friends to gauge their interest. To my surprise, they all agreed and thought it sounded like a fun idea.

We've been getting together every month to discuss books across multiple genres including personal development, psychology and spirituality. It has been an amazing experience, and my friendships have deepened because of it.

As Napoleon Hill suggests in *Think & Grow Rich*, "No two minds ever come together without, thereby, creating a third, invisible, intangible force which may be likened to a third mind."[1]

Something magical happens when two or more people get together to share ideas, especially when there is a common purpose. You tap into a collective wisdom of sorts that isn't available when you're isolated and learning alone.

Is there a local book club you could join in your area? If not, would it make sense to start your own?

Leveraging Technology

In this Information Age, you don't necessarily have to meet in person.

If local meetings don't exist, or if meeting in person isn't your thing, you have plenty of other options. Even when you find yourself living in the middle of a pandemic, there are still communities of like-minded people congregating online.

In fact, since I originally wrote this chapter, the coronavirus pandemic has quarantined the entire world, but I feel more connected than ever to the communities I'm involved with thanks to technology.

You can even join "groups" on your favorite social media platforms. Last month, I reread one of my favorite books of all time and wanted to connect with other people who enjoy this book as much as I do. I found study groups for this exact book on both Facebook and LinkedIn. After joining them, I've found a lot of value in participating in the conversation.

What are you learning right now? Would joining an online group dedicated to this topic benefit you in any way? If so, search for these groups on your favorite social media platform; you'll be amazed at what's out there.

Like the extracurricular activities you participated in during school, joining communities of like-minded people in the real world can help you take your learning and growth to an entirely new level. Participating in these communities will also help you advance toward your goals much faster than you could on your own.

Key Points

- Surrounding ourselves with like-minded people is just as important in the real world as it was in school. By doing so, you not only take your learning and growth to an entirely new level, but you also advance toward your goals much faster than you can on your own.
- Most cities offer memberships, associations, clubs and classes of like-minded people you could join.
- Meeting frequently with a friend for the purpose of holding one another accountable can help you (and your friend) stay on track toward accomplishing your goals.
- Book clubs can be a great way to connect on a mutual topic of interest and deepen relationships.
- Something magical happens when two or more people get together to share ideas, especially when there is a common purpose. You tap into a collective wisdom of

sorts that isn't available if you're isolated and learning alone.

- If local meetings don't exist, or if meeting in person isn't your thing, you have plenty of other options. Even when you find yourself living in the middle of a pandemic, there are still communities of like-minded people congregating online.

Chapter Assignment

1. Are there any memberships, associations, clubs, or classes you could join in your local area? If so, consider joining one of these communities over the next few weeks.
2. Do you struggle with your commitments? If so, consider asking a friend if he or she would like to meet frequently for the purpose of holding one another accountable.
3. Is there a local book club you could join in your area? If not, would it make sense to start your own?
4. Are there online communities you could join on Facebook, LinkedIn, or other social media platforms that relate back to an area of interest? If so, consider joining and contributing to the conversation over the next few weeks.

CONCLUSION: WILL YOU PASS OR FAIL?

"There is nothing more tragic than to come to the end of life and know we have been on the wrong course."

— WATCHMAN NEE

In our final moments, I believe we're going to wonder whether we *passed* or *failed* at this beautiful thing we call "life."

If this is true, what steps can we take, right now, to give us that *inner knowing* that we'll pass life's final examination?

A great place to start is by following the approach described in this book. This is the exact same approach that radically transformed my life ten years ago, and it continues to guide my life in a meaningful way today.

I am confident that this approach, if followed carefully, will forever change the trajectory of your life just as it has for so many of the individuals and groups I've been blessed to serve over the years.

You *can* break free from conventional wisdom and live life on *your* terms instead.

How to Apply this Book

I want you to seriously consider if this is the right approach for you. Will it help you at this stage of your life? Will it help you based on your unique circumstances? Does it align well with your own personal values and beliefs?

If the answer is "yes," I encourage you to be more intentional about applying the lessons within this book by *scheduling them*.

For your convenience, here's an estimate regarding how much time it'll take to reread each chapter and complete the assignments. This is based both on my own personal experience as well as the experiences of my clients.

- Chapter 1: Subject Areas (1.5 hours)
- Chapter 2: Progress Reports (1.5 hours)
- Chapter 3: Homework Assignments (2 hours)
- Chapter 4: Lockers & Backpacks (7 hours)
- Chapter 5: Study Hall (2 hours)
- Chapter 6: Structured Days (1.5 hours)
- Chapter 7: Classroom Environments (4 hours)
- Chapter 8: Majors, Minors & Electives (2 hours)
- Chapter 9: Lesson Plans (4 hours)
- Chapter 10: Retreats (2 hours)
- Chapter 11: Office Hours (4 hours)
- Chapter 12: Extracurricular Activities (4 hours)

I'd encourage you to apply the teachings in this book at whatever speed works best for you. Based on your existing time capacity, there are several ways you could proceed.

- Read and apply one chapter per month for twelve months
- Read and apply one chapter per week for twelve weeks (recommended)
- Read and apply two chapters per week for six weeks
- Read and apply one chapter per day for twelve days (not recommended)

Based on the feedback I've received from my clients over the years, the twelve-week timeline produces the best results.

Taking into consideration your existing schedule and commitments, which timeline works best for you?

Once you've made your decision, schedule it in your calendar *immediately*.

Also, be sure to access all the free resources mentioned within this book at IntentionalBook.com.

It has been a real honor and a privilege to be your guide on this very unique and exciting journey. If there's anything else I can do to support you, please send me an email directly: sean@seanrosensteel.com.

As the late Wayne Dyer used to say, *"I send you love and all green lights."*

ENDNOTES

Introduction: Why Conventional Wisdom is a Trap

1. Carl Jung, *Collected Works of C.G. Jung* (Princeton: Princeton University Press, 2000), Volume 7: 115.
2. Dr. Wayne W. Dyer, *The Shift: Taking Your Life from Ambition to Meaning* (Carlsbad: Hay House Inc., 2019).

3. Homework Assignments

1. Gary Keller, *The One Thing: The Surprisingly Simple Truth Behind Extraordinary Results* (Austin: Bard Press, 2012), 106.

4. Lockers & Backpacks

1. Darby E. Saxbe, Rena Repetti, "No Place Like Home: Home tours correlate with daily patterns of mood and cortisol," *University of California*, November 23, 2009, https://pubmed.ncbi.nlm.nih.gov/19934011/.
2. Napoleon Hill, *Think and Grow Rich* (New York: Fall River Press, 2012), 48.
3. David Allen, *Getting Things Done: The Art of Stress-Free Productivity* (London: Penguin Books, 2015).
4. Ryder Carrol, *The Bullet Journal Method* (London: Fourth Estate, 2018).
5. Tony Robbins, The Time of Your Life (Los Angeles: Westlake Entertainment, 2009).
6. Deepak Chopra, "Why Meditate?," *The Chopra Center*, September 24, 2013, https://www.deepakchopra.com/blog/article/4701.

5. Study Hall

1. Brian Tracy, *Master Your Time, Master Your Life: The Breakthrough System to Get More Results, Faster, in Every Area of Your Life* (New York: Tarcher-Perigee, 2016), 56.
2. James Clear, *Atomic Habits: An Easy & Proven Way to Build Good Habits & Break Bad Ones* (New York: Avery, 2018), 108.

6. Structured Days

1. Darren Hardy, *The Compound Effect* (New York: First Vanguard Press, 2010), 10.
2. Stephen Covey, *The 7 Habits of Highly Effective People* (New York: Simon & Schuster, 2013), 170.

7. Classroom Environments

1. Amy He, Average US Time Spent with Mobile in 2019 Has Increased, *eMarketer*, June 4, 2019, https://www.emarketer.com/content/average-us-time-spent-with-mobile-in-2019-has-increased.
2. Daniel J. Levitin, *The Organized Mind: Thinking Straight in the Age of Information Overload,* (New York: Dutton, 2016), 101.

8. Majors, Minors & Electives

1. Viktor E. Frankl, *Man's Search for Meaning* (Boston: Beacon Press, 2006), 106.
2. *Encyclopedia Britannica,* s.v. "Physiology," (Encyclopedia Britannica Inc., 2020). https://www.britannica.com/science/information-theory/Physiology.

9. Lesson Plans

1. Dr. Wayne W. Dyer, *Change Your Thoughts, Change Your Life: Living the Wisdom of the Tao* (Carlsbad: Hay House Inc., 2007), 302.
2. FranklinCovey, "Big Rocks," YouTube Video, 4:01, August 24, 2017, https://youtu.be/zV3gMTOEWt8.
3. Napoleon Hill, *Think and Grow Rich* (New York: Fall River Press, 2012), 72.

10. Retreats

1. Stephen Covey, *How to Develop Your Personal Mission Statement* (Seattle: Grand Harbor Press, 2013). Retrieved from https://www.amazon.com/Develop-Your-Personal-Mission-Statement-ebook/dp/B00CWIK2I8.

11. Office Hours

1. TJ McCue, E Learning Climbing To $325 Billion By 2025 UF Canvas Absorb Schoology Moodle, *Forbes*, July 31, 2018, https://www.forbes.com/sites/tjmccue/2018/07/31/e-learning-climbing-to-325-billion-by-2025-uf-canvas-absorb-schoology-moodle/.
2. Dave Ramsey, *The Total Money Makeover: A Proven Plan for Financial Fitness* (Nashville, Thomas Nelson, 2013).
3. Gary Chapman, *The 5 Love Languages: The Secret to Love that Lasts* (Chicago: Northfield Publishing, 2014).
4. Tony Robbins, Ultimate Relationship Program (Los Angeles: Westlake Entertainment, 2009).

12. Extracurricular Activities

1. Napoleon Hill, *Think and Grow Rich* (New York: Fall River Press, 2012), 125.

ACKNOWLEDGMENTS

This book would not have been possible without the love and support of so many people.

Thank you to my loving wife, Karen. Once again, you put your full faith and trust in me. You gave me the autonomy to pursue my dream of becoming an author, and I'm forever grateful. I'm so thankful for all of your support and for taking such incredible care of our children while I've been locked away these past few months. It gives me great peace of mind knowing they're in such loving and capable hands. You're an amazing wife and such an incredibly loving mother. You'll always be my Superwoman.

Thank you to my three beautiful children, Oliver, Alice and Henry. You're my greatest teachers, and I continue learning so much from you every day. Please promise me you'll never, ever grow up...just keep growing.

A big thanks to my mom and dad, Tom and Nuala. Words cannot express my appreciation for your unconditional love. Thank you for standing by me in my darkest hours and for encouraging me to take charge of my life and figure things out for myself. You've set the standard for exceptional parenting, and my children will be the true benefactors of all the sacrifices you've made for us throughout your lifetimes.

For my aunt Marge. You mean so much to my family and me. Thank you for being so generous to us over the years. I hope you know we're your biggest fans.

For my three older siblings, Amy, Tommy and Tracy. Each of you has contributed greatly to my life in unique ways, and I wouldn't be who I am today without you.

To my mother-in-law, Susie. Thank you for contributing so profoundly to our family. I'll forever be grateful for your unwavering support for Karen, the kiddos and me.

I owe much gratitude to my siblings-in-law, Keith, Jennifer, Dan, Meagan and Amanda. Keith, thank you for your continued support and encouragement. It's fun to be on a parallel path and help one another along the way. Dan and Meagan, thank you for allowing me to write over these past few months from your beautiful home during this pandemic. Amanda, thank you for being one of the early guinea pigs of this approach. The feedback you so generously provided has been invaluable.

Thank you to all my friends who have helped me along this journey, especially Matt Brown, Jay Rodgers, Dr. Connor LaVallie, Michael Schultz, Nick Palczynski, Michael Cohen, Michelle Bottino, Shaun Schroeder, Al Ritter, Bo Smith, Jim Di Ciaula, Dave Tamkin, Tiza Pyle, Drago Gudovic, Jon LoDuca, Keith Wollenberg, Ken Cromwell, Greg Cibura, Jana Roe, Kenny William and Scott Piner.

Thank you to all my clients and students who have allowed me to serve them over the years. Without your faith, trust, feedback and encouragement, this book would not be possible.

To my amazingly talented editors, James Cook and C.J. Anaya. Thank you both for your unwavering patience on numerous occasions when I was struggling to organize and clarify my thoughts .

Special thanks to Jelena Mirkovic Jankovic, the most talented and understanding designer I've ever have the privilege to work with.

A big shout out to the many mentors who have guided me on my path, especially Wayne Dyer, Brendon Burchard, Eckhart Tolle, Tony Robbins, Deepak Chopra, Bruce Lipton, Paulo Coelho, Napoleon Hill, Michael Singer and Stephen Covey.

And finally, thank you to Ms. Davis, my freshman-year English teacher. While I was penalized for my handwriting in other classes, you encouraged me by explaining that combining the printed letter with cursive was a sign of brilliance. Your encouragement meant a lot to me back then, and it continues to mean a lot to me to this day.

ABOUT THE AUTHOR

Sean Rosensteel is an author and the founder of The Intentional Living Academy.

With a passion for helping others, Sean's journey began when he found himself bankrupt at the age of 28 after following conventional wisdom all his life. This eye-opening moment taught him that attaining true happiness and fulfillment means breaking free of societal chains and creating your own path.

Now, he hopes to inspire and empower his readers to achieve their dreams and live the lives they truly deserve.

Sean currently lives in the Dallas, TX area with his loving wife, Karen, and their three young children.

For more information visit www.SeanRosensteel.com.

CPSIA information can be obtained
at www.ICGtesting.com
Printed in the USA
LVHW041423280720
661663LV00013B/195/J